W9-ARS-987
Ch. 1 - Wednesday
Act. 1 Wed -- p. 19 manual

FREE TO FIGHT BACK
A Self Defense Handbook
for Women

FREE to FIGHT BACK

A SELF-DEFENSE HANDBOOK FOR WOMEN

text & illustrations by
MARILYN SCRIBNER

Harold Shaw Publishers
Wheaton, Illinois

Copyright © 1988 by Marilyn Scribner

All rights reserved. No part of this book may be reproduced or transmitted in any form or by any means, electronic or mechanical, including photocopying, recording, or any information storage and retrieval system, without written permission from Harold Shaw Publishers, Box 567, Wheaton, Illinois 60189. Printed in the United States of America.

ISBN 0-87788-285-1

Library of Congress Cataloging-in-Publication Data
Scribner, Marilyn.
    Free to fight back : a self-defense handbook for women / Marilyn Scribner.
        p. cm.
    Bibliography: p.
    Includes index.
    ISBN 0-87788-285-1
    1. Women—Crimes against. 2. Self-defense for women. I. Title.
HV6250.4W65S36 1988
613.6′6′024042—dc19   88-19780
                                                                      CIP

---

97 96 95 94 93 92 91 90 89 88

10 9 8 7 6 5 4 3 2 1

To Marcia
A friend in all seasons

Contents

Acknowledgments

I would like to thank my friends and family,
who kept asking, "When will the book be done?";
Margaret Aitken, my friend and college professor mentor;
Beth Tanis, for typing.
I extend my deepest appreciation
to Marcia Hurt who edited,
encouraged, prodded, and collaborated with me
throughout the writing of this book.

Introduction

The Christian church in America has certainly had its share of problems. Not only does the church work against forces from without, but it also deals with numerous internal problems. Congregational strife, continuous building programs, board selections, church socials, and the eternal decision as to who will be the choir director have too often occupied enormous amounts of the church's energy. Without realizing it, a church or group can become encumbered with these concerns and lose its perspective regarding significant and broader issues.

One area that the church in America has sorely neglected is attention to local and global social injustices. For the most part, churches have perceived themselves as separate from these social matters and have concentrated primarily on internal growth and evangelism. Because of this stand, the church in general does not exist as a liberating force against social bondage. It conveys a mixed message to the secular world. When humanity claims to be interested in truth, freedom, and justice for all, can the church afford to be any less concerned?

Most groups or organizations which isolate themselves from society at large begin to stagnate and wither. The Jim Jones cult stands as an extreme example of such total exclusiveness. Jones's followers ultimately lost contact with reality, wasting hundreds of lives in a wave of death and destruction.

Of course there are extremes in both directions. One church might not care for social, global problems at all, while another holds social concerns as its highest priority and neglects evangelism and nurturing the individual Christian within the church. Either system falls far short of the great commission of evangelism given by the Lord.

The most horrendous moral and physical crime of recent history was committed against the Jewish people during the holocaust. Most of the world claimed they did not know of the suffering that occurred. Where was the Christian church during that evil time? The church's response should have resounded in unified uproar throughout the world. God help us if we knew and did not try to do anything about it.

Where were American Christians during the race revolution in the '60s? They did not come to the forefront of freedom and equality during the civil rights struggle. Rather, many Christians participated in opposition, to keep blacks "in their place." Too many churches excluded these children of God from their church services, and some still do.

The church is still hesitant to deal with social problems. Critical issues such as rape, pornography, child abuse, divorce, abortion, drugs, and abandonment of the elderly have shocked some churches to their senses. And the whole question of the value of women—personally, and in the church—is one of the last subjects some churches want to discuss.

In both the race and the gender movements, it has been the *secular world* which sought freedom for people—not the church. Many churches have kept women from using their gifts and abilities in the church with the same freedoms men experience. But informed and godly people are not accepting an inferior place for women in the church anymore.

As ardent Christians, we must choose to look at issues or situations the way we believe God looks at them. Would God want Jewish people to be slaughtered? Would he want blacks to be enslaved? Would he want children to be abused? Would God want women to be beaten, raped, and humiliated? The answer is clear—No! God left Christians here on earth to restrain the power of evil. The Christian world should realize that God's love for all of his creatures is incorporated in the heart of evangelism. And Christians *must be aware* of his hatred of a cruel and unjust society. God's mandate to the church is to bring a hurting world into a realization and knowledge of himself. If God is who he says he is, then he loves that which is good, hates that which is bad, and charges the church to follow his lead.

What does all this have to do with self defense for women? This book deals with skills and techniques of defense, but it also deals with attitudes. Why are women assaulted and humiliated? It starts with an incorrect attitude about women: they are less worthy and can be dominated. A negative attitude sets the stage for women to be easily victimized, deprived of freedom, assaulted, and perhaps brutalized. If a woman is continuously kept under tyrannical male leadership which represses her mentality and abilities, neither she nor those around her will place a significant value on her. When attacks come against her, she will be unsure of her skills and may question whether she is actually worth defending. This book will deal not only with assault and attacks to a woman's body, but also to a woman's self-esteem and societal value.

This book is about assaults against women and how women have been historically programmed to feel that such abuse is their destiny. The good news is that men and women can change that system of attitudes! Every woman should be informed of new choices, new rights, and new freedoms from fear. Victim or victor? You can choose.

Marilyn Scribner

1
What's Your View of Women?

WHY SHOULD A BOOK ON SELF DEFENSE BEGIN WITH A discussion on the biblical, the historical, and the godly view of women? Because an attitude about women comes into play when a rapist is looking for a victim to dominate. And some attitudes about women make women victims feel unworthy or unable to defend themselves. Those same attitudes about women make it hard for those of us outside the assault situation to understand it clearly. So transforming our view of women is the best place for a book about self defense to begin.

A look into the past is the best way to get a clear picture of the dilemma that faces women of today. When did the idea of second-class citizenship for women come into being? Why is it that 99 percent of today's rapes (at least those reported) occur against women? Why are women hesitant to be aggressive in defending themselves? Is there a correlation between society's view of the woman and how she values herself? Is there a correlation between self-worth and self defense?

A Historic View of Women

Old Testament times

The pattern for society's treatment of women was determined early—in the garden of Eden. When God decided that Adam could not live by himself, he created Eve. From these events, some conclude that God created his best first. And others argue that God's greatest and highest act was his final one—the creation of woman. The significance of the order of creation can be argued both ways. It is difficult to believe that an all-knowing God created Eve merely as an afterthought. Some people have construed God's creation term "helper" to mean servant rather than equal. It is amazing how much of today's behavior toward women in the church is based on guesswork about the creation process.

And, to make matters worse, since Eve first ate of the forbidden fruit, woman has forever taken the blame for influencing Adam to do the same. Adam could have refused the fruit; he did not. He even attempted to excuse himself, "The woman made me do it!" Then he used Eve to rationalize his disobedience and got a shot at God as well: "The woman that YOU gave me!"

We now know the terrible consequences of that act by those two people who shared in creation, shared in sin, and shared in the consequences of disobedience to God. God announced their judgment: they were barred from the garden. Adam's lot was to toil, and Eve's was to serve the rest of her life. Were these pronouncements a command or a prophecy? Eve's judgment has proven to be prophetically true: Christian and non-Christian women alike have served down through the ages.

But those of us who are redeemed have turned away from the judgment of sin in the garden and have come back, through Christ, into fellowship with the Father as though the fall had not occurred. The declaration of punishment is no longer in effect for those who believe in the Lord Jesus Christ and his work of redemption on the cross. God has called us to serve each other; a woman should not be called on to be more of a servant than a man.

The Old Testament gives us a shameful picture of women in Hebrew society. For the most part, women were considered chattel, property of their fathers. Then they were transferred for a price to become the property of their husbands. A woman had little status, few rights, and probably no part in the selection of her husband.

The Old Testament reveals an amazing viewpoint regarding attitudes toward women who had been raped. Unbelievably, in some cases the assault of a woman was considered to be her fault. Rape was also a means of revenge, restitution, and bargaining. The Scriptures relate some consequences for a raped woman.

If a virgin was raped out in the country, monetary restitution was made to the father. But if a virgin was raped in the city, both parties were killed. Since no one in the city had heard her scream, the victim was assumed to be guilty of a sexual sin. *Deuteronomy 22:23-24*

If an attacker of a raped virgin was found, he had to pay the father fifty shekels and marry the girl. *Deuteronomy 22:28-30*

When Dinah was raped, her brothers avenged her by bargaining with the rapist for land and possessions. Later, her brothers killed the rapist. *Genesis 34*

A virgin daughter was offered to men in order to defer homosexual abuse of a guest. *Judges 19*

Little is recorded about the needs or feelings of the victim; her father was the injured party. The early Talmud also directed that a raped woman had to marry the rapist. Eventually a change was made, and fifty coins were allowed to pay for her damage. According to early Assyrian laws, the father of a raped person had the right to rape the rapist's wife. Even the selection and choosing of a bride was sometimes done by rape.

New Testament times

If New Testament times were better for women, it wasn't very noticeable. The attitudes of Old Testament days still prevailed.

John 8 tells of a woman brought to Jesus who had been caught in the act of adultery. The scribes and Pharisees maintained that by the law of Moses she was to be stoned. Considering she was caught "in the act" of adultery, it's odd that there is no mention of the man who was caught with her. It was a double standard; only the woman was guilty.

Women still served men. Holy men prayed every day, thanking God that they were not born as women. While some female names begin to emerge in responsible places of leadership, there is relatively little evidence of their prominence in local church activities. Scripture passages encourage women to be quiet in the churches (which indicates their level of participation in church functions).

Church history tells us that women were not educated nor well read in Hebrew society. Since they were uninformed and uninvolved in the church agenda, they were relegated to the back part of the meeting place. Separated and bored, the women talked noisily and distracted the men involved in the meetings. This explains Paul's direction for them to be quiet in church and ask their husbands about the meetings when they got home. This hebraic direction has figuratively kept females in the back of churches until today, hiding the abilities and spiritual gifts of women through the years.

What if we took Paul's cultural statement, "Slaves, obey your masters" literally today? We would still have slavery! If other cultural directions were literally obeyed, we could never wear gold jewelry or attend church without wearing a hat. It is rather hypocritical for churches to select only a few cultural directives of the New Testament to enforce.

Recent history

Martin Luther was a great theologian, but he didn't know much about anthropology. He once declared that men should do all of the thinking because they had big heads and broad shoulders. And he thought that because women had little heads and wide hips, they should stay at home, bear children, and not try to think. That didn't help to clear up the problems of women!

Early English laws were damaging for women as well. Women all over the world must have been thrilled when, after a bitter debate, the English parliament finally decided that women did have souls after all. Equally ridiculous, but tied to Old Testament times, was the continuing debate in parliament as to whether rape was a criminal act against the person or a violation of the man's property.

In the 1940's Freud set women back by his psychoanalysis of them as silly and neurotic. He based his conclusions regarding female frustration on the tenet of male envy. Apparently it did not occur to him that, while the frustrations were real, women did not want to be men; they wanted to be free *like* men.

A Current View of Women

In the church

It's disappointing to discover that the majority of churches are run mostly by men. We've held on to the "women-don't-teach-be-silent" culture of early church times. What a loss for the church! What a waste of skills, talents, and God-given gifts that could have been used for his glory. Too many churches today are functioning with the same organizational structure as in Bible times. Women are allowed to be Sunday school teachers, but they do not preach, usher, take up the offering, or serve communion. It's sad that so many sisters in Christ cannot share in those experiences. Churches which hold the position that women cannot participate in leadership activities run into trouble when no man is available to do the job.

The mission field is surprisingly free from such restrictions. Mission fields are disproportionately served by women. Their roles often include administration, preaching, and serving communion. Why is this service permissible on the mission field and not in home churches?

So what do women do with their natural resources and talents in leadership that are not used within the high level of church organization? Let's look at an example. A woman who is the vice-president of a large Chicago bank is also the treasurer of her suburban church. However, because she is female, she is allowed only to work with the books and cannot directly handle the money. What a wasted resource of talent!

And who is permitted to do religious counseling in American churches? When I had been a Christian for forty-three years, I was told by a male Christian of five years that he could not accept any spiritual guidance or insight from a female because he was the authority figure. He steadfastly believed that God reveals himself to women through men. But God has made it clear that he looks on the heart and not the outward appearance. It is difficult to imagine that he chooses to confine himself to one set of reproductive organs over another.

Do we honestly believe that the gospel is diminished or communion is less worshipful because a woman has administered it? When you are passed the bread and the cup, does it matter who does the passing? Communion is a time for all hearts to be lifted to God in worship. We know gender is not going to be a factor in heaven, so why have we so locked ourselves into role playing here on earth? Assigning tasks according to gifts and talents would be much more productive for the church.

If we want to take Scripture seriously, then we must honestly look at Galatians 3:28: "There is neither Jew nor Greek, there is neither slave nor free, there is neither male nor female: for you are all one in Christ Jesus." That is total equality.

God's View of Women

All persons, both men and women, have a tendency to view themselves as others see them. External qualities such as appearance, job status, salary, type of car(s), location of residence, and charitable work help to formulate an internal self-value system. This mirroring of outward attributes for establishing a worthy identity breaks down under God's scrutiny. He acknowledges worthiness in people who are faithful to him, obedient, and loyal in service with the talents and gifts given to them.

So how does God view women? Look at Genesis 1:26: "Let us make man (not *a* man) in our image, after our likeness, and let *them* rule over . . . all the earth" (italics added). It can be safely assumed that women were part of the original planning of God. A woman was not given lesser intelligence and fewer gifts than man received. It is natural that she should want to create, lead, initiate, and give back to God all of her gifts.

In developing the redemption process, there is never the slightest implication that God designed a program of salvation that did not include women. The good news for women in the New Testament is that Christ dealt with women in the same way he would with a man. He condemned their sin and still showed tenderness toward them. He dealt with Mary and Martha with love (Luke 10:38-42; John 11). He did not condemn the adulterous woman who was to be stoned but told her to go and not sin again (John 8:3-11). With the woman at the well, he not only crossed the racial barrier by speaking to a Samaritan, but he also crossed a social barrier by speaking to a *woman* (John 4:7-26).

Each Christian woman can stand before the Lord and believe that she has full rights and responsibilities before him. She is a whole person fully redeemed by the blood of Christ.

The Scripture never indicates that only one of the species was to be indwelt by the Holy Spirit. As part of Christ's redemptive work, there is a clear statement that God's Spirit is a gift to *all* believers. It is this Spirit which supplies spiritual gifts to both genders. Coincidentally, the attributes which are typically considered female characteristics—gentleness, love, kindness, meekness, patience, longsuffering—are the characteristics which describe the fruits of the Spirit of God (Galatians 5:22-23).

So what does all this mean? It means that a woman is not a tagalong human being—even when time and circumstances have convinced her that she *is* a second-class citizen. Yet the civilized world still acts out its misconceptions about the woman's role in a church society and uses Scripture to back them up. I cannot question the truth of Scripture. But I *do* question the ability of people to distinguish proclamations from cultural directives. Women were created by God the Father, died for by the Son, and are the temple of the living God. She should now be free—free from fear and bondage, and free to defend herself.

Feeling good about yourself and your womanhood and being assured of your place in God's family is important to self defense because it prepares you to take care of what is valuable to yourself and to the Lord: you! A transformation of negative attitudes is the foundation of self defense for Christian women.

2

The Way It Is

I'M SURE I DON'T NEED TO REMIND YOU THAT THE WORLD IS NOT a perfect place. You have more than enough reminders! The kitchen sink clogs just when company is about to arrive. You make a mistake in your checkbook and bounce an important check. The car won't start when you have five minutes to make it to church on time. Often it even hurts to watch the evening news broadcast. Sometimes our machines fail us, our friends fail us, and we fail ourselves. That's the way it is.

It's terrible, but it's not surprising that issues of assault and rape and self defense are clouded with some misconceptions and some problem attitudes. But we can keep a positive spirit and do our best to set things straight.

The Way It Is—Socially

The prevalent belief in society today is that men have been and always will be the woman's protector. This notion stems from past years when women worked at home in the house or on the farm with fathers, sons, and husbands close at hand in the family fields. Women were in contact with male protection for most of the day. But because of our progressive, professional, and mobile society, such family clustering no longer exists. Since the female population now comprises more than 50 percent of the work force, the home is not the place of protection it once was. And the large majority of men are out of the home during the day as well. Even if women were to stay at home in a place of so-called security, they are not necessarily no longer at risk. An emerging statistic reveals that most rapes occur during home invasion. A person in today's society who believes that the male can take care of the woman twenty-four hours a day is either naive or unwilling to accept reality.

Society and the law support the self-defense concept. People are becoming more and more frustrated with a legal system that seems to have broken down under the weight of enormous criminal activity. Increasing crime rates, coupled with a staggering legal system, render us vulnerable to attack. It is imperative that we help one another prevent crime. Unfortunately, in many cases that have been reported, onlookers witnessed beatings, stabbings, rape, and even murder without so much as a phone call to the police to assist the victim. The recurring theme in these cases always runs the same: "I didn't want to get involved."

The most famous case in point took place on a sidewalk in New York. A woman was repeatedly stabbed and ultimately killed within the immediate view and hearing of more than thirty people. During the assault she screamed for help. Incredibly, no one came to her aid; no one even bothered to call the police. Again, their reason was that they just didn't want to get involved in someone else's problems.

The philosopher Edmund Burke made this well-known statement: "All that is necessary for the triumph of evil is that good men should do nothing." A community of people can never be stronger than its resolved resistance to evil, crime, disease, ignorance, poverty, and injustice. For the church and for mankind, the issue of attack against women is part of its strength or its weakness. We have the right and the responsibility to build a society that is free from fear and personal destruction for each of its members.

The Way It Is —Legally

Historically, we have expected the law to protect us from crime. In fact, a solid belief in enforcement of law and order is a significant factor in the election of our governing officials. We idealistically believe that when we pay our taxes, we are paying for protection from assaults. But now we are dealing with criminal activity so prevalent that we can no longer be assured of safety.

The legal system is overburdened with ever-increasing crime rates. Law enforcement officers simply cannot be everywhere, and consequently criminal activity has ballooned beyond the total effectiveness of the law. To make matters worse, the judicial and enforcement systems have not been effective in the areas of rehabilitation. The repeating criminal has not been kept off the streets. For instance, the rapist is usually a continual repeater of his crime. Studies clearly indicate that once a man begins a rape pattern, he cannot stop himself; he will not quit until he is caught. And even if he is caught, the ratio of conviction for a rapist is very low—about one conviction in twenty-five cases. Obviously, the courts have neither the means nor the capacity to control this particular crime adequately.

Reporting a rape is extremely difficult for the victim. Reporting a burglary or robbery is not. If your television is stolen, you report the crime to the police and it will likely be recorded as a fact. But the report of a rape is usually referred to as an "alleged rape." The victim of rape assault will be expected to answer such questions as: "Do you have a witness?" and, "Did you struggle?" Or, in the case of female rape, "Was he your boyfriend?" and, "How were you dressed?" Rape victims have even been asked, "Did you enjoy it?" in an attempt to determine the veracity of the story.

Fortunately, it is now considered illegal to conduct such an interview with a victim. The problem is currently being treated more humanely with the addition of specially trained police officers, some of which are women. Pressure by women's groups organized against rape has been a force in effecting a more professional handling of rape reporting. After a rape assault, a woman often does not want a male police officer interviewing her, especially if insensitive questions with accompanying innuendoes are asked. Today a victim has the right to request the presence of a female police officer while giving her statement regarding the assault.

Difficulty in reporting the rape assault is further complicated when there is no visible sign of a struggle on the part of the victim. If a person does not appear beaten or show signs of bruises and other abuses, she loses credibility regarding the attack. Women have received conflicting advice about methods for responding to attack. Sometimes they have been told not to fight back; if they do, they might be killed. On the other hand, if she doesn't struggle, she is not believed when she reports the crime. The theory of not fighting back has a major flaw in it: there is no guarantee that the victim will not be killed even if she cooperates with the attacker. Richard Speck, who killed eight nurses, reported that none of the women offered any resistance. Rape often includes murder.

Another legal problem is the reluctance of the victim to appear in court. While on the witness stand, a victim must relive the attack in grisly detail within the view and hearing of everyone in the courtroom. The testimony is followed by grueling cross-examination by the defense lawyer, who attempts to discredit the testimony of the victim. This process is emotionally damaging to the already injured victim. So, because of the trauma of the interrogation and a low conviction ratio in rape cases, most lawyers encourage their clients to accept a lesser plea by the accused.

Even so, while the court system has formerly been found wanting in the rape solution, there has been some progress in legal areas. There is new pressure for swifter and surer convictions to eliminate trials and retrials that go on to the point of exhaustion. The laws of this land value a woman's right to defend herself swiftly and vigorously during an attack. In most states, a woman has the right to defend herself to the point of the death of the attacker, if necessary. The law grants people the right to defend themselves when threatened with death or rape without punishment.

Generally, older dictionaries have defined rape as forced sexual intercourse when one party is unwilling for the act to occur. But the word "intercourse" has no place in the reality of rape. "Intercourse" means an interchange between two parties with the implication of equal exchange and mutual consent. The term hardly applies to the rape act when the woman fights with her whole being to avoid the encounter.

The use of the word "sexual" is also misleading. Its connotations lead to myths and fallacies. Attaching the word "sexual" to rape minimizes the violence—as though the behavior is not aberrant. Fortunately, some state legislatures have recently re-identified the definition of rape by deleting the words "sexual" and "intercourse." These laws now also include a much larger range of physical practices which are characterized as acts of rape.

Let's take legislation from my home state as an example. The Illinois Criminal Sexual Assault Law of 1984 (information from the Illinois Coalition Against Sexual Assault) introduces some new definitions and new penalties. These are a few of them:

- Rapists of all ages and both sexes have to be considered sex offenders. Juveniles under fourteen may be prosecuted, and males and females can be charged with sex crimes.

- Spouses who sexually assault their partners can no longer be excluded from the law. Spouses may be prosecuted in certain cases of sexual assault.

- Penalties for sex crimes involving young children have been increased. Sexual assault of a child under thirteen has the most serious penalty.

- Victims can no longer be required to fight off the attacker. A victim does not have to resist to prove that she or he did not consent to sexual violence.

To Fight or Not to Fight?

The whole issue of resistance to violence presents a problem for some Christians. First of all, women generally do not know how to respond to physical confrontations because of their cultural upbringing. Observation of any elementary school playground will reveal most little boys in rough and tumble play, while the girls are involved in jump rope or "hopscotch" type games. Boys are taught to fight early in life ("boys will be boys"), while their female counterparts learn early that "nice little girls don't fight."

Ideally no one should have to learn to fight. But realistically, little girls should learn to fight early as well. It is ironic that the gender which *needs* to learn to fight early is the one that does not. Because she has limited skills, an assault confrontation temporarily paralyzes the victim with fright. The good news is that it is possible to change the pattern.

Second, some people believe that to react physically or to defend yourself is "unChristian." They derive their opinion from the injunction to "turn the other cheek." Although "turn the other cheek" applies to most relational situations, this troubling viewpoint can also allow wrongdoing to run rampant and unchecked. One of the Christian's responsibilities is to restrain evil in a fallen world. Evil will not restrain itself— external resistance is necessary. Throughout the Old Testament, God used his people to restrain those who were evil and offensive to him. Brutal beatings, rapes, and murders are not only violent acts against God's creatures, but they offend the holy nature of God himself.

When the ultimate goal is to thwart an attack, the immediate goal is to cause pain to the attacker. This reaction by the "victim" should not be construed as wrongdoing or returning evil for evil, but should be considered an act of resistance. Pain says, "Stop doing what you are doing." If successful, such a message keeps evil from occurring. Even though there are different levels of pain recognition, pain is a universal language. Even a small child has a clear concept of what a spanking means. Granted, the infliction of pain is a temporary stopgap method, but the pain message is understood. Self-defense skills use the same premise. The pain must be severe enough to stop and, hopefully, immobilize the attacker.

For anyone who believes they can talk their way out of an attack situation, remember this: there are many raped and/or dead women who thought the same thing. Talking is certainly one possible means of defense, but it is extremely unreliable by itself. How do you determine what statements are reasonable to someone drunk, on drugs, or crazed? It is critical for every man, woman, and child to acquire the physical skills that can inhibit brutal acts.

The other side of the pain issue is your own reaction to physical pain. Be assured that if an attack is imminent, there will certainly be pain involved. So it is beneficial to program your mind about the matter of pain reception. Research indicates that people react differently to similar pain stimuli. Some have been able to subdue and control pain receptors biomechanically by mentally rejecting the pain sensation.

Try this simple experiment. Take a fold of skin on your arm between your thumb and index finger. Pinch it and twist it very hard. Let it hurt! Now find another spot on your arm and do it again. When it becomes extremely painful, tell yourself out loud, "It does not hurt. It does not hurt." Once you have mentally gained control of the pain, pinch and twist even harder, and repeat louder and longer that it does not hurt. Totally *reject* the pain by refusing to acknowledge it mentally. When under attack, a person who is able to control pain is much more free to respond to the attack with a clear mind and singleness of purpose.

For You and for Others

Once you get past the question, "*Could* I defend myself?" the next question is, "*Should* I?" It would probably be better to reverse those two questions. But, regardless of the sequence, when dealing with the necessity for preventive self defense and actual skills in self defense, a woman needs to resolve that she will do everything within her power to thwart an attack against her body or to defend a loved one.

God has built a survival instinct into our physical structure. If I trip and fall, my hands instinctively go out to protect myself and to cushion the fall. The desire to survive runs deep inside us. You may be surprised at what you can do. People who say, "I could never do that" are mistaken. When an attack comes, they find they will fight with everything they have to survive. And knowing some techniques for self defense is intelligent survival. Beating on an attacker's chest is not constructive defense, but beating on his nose is. It helps to know these things *before* the actual attack.

All people, but especially Christians, have a responsibility to help those around them. You might not feel that you can fight for yourself, but could you stand by and watch someone beat on your mother or hurt your little brother or sister? To defend them, you should be able to strike with purpose and accuracy.

A society which takes a passive attitude of not getting involved and not attempting to stand against violence is one which eventually will lose the battle of freedom from fear. Even today people hide in their homes for fear of being hurt and violated. Learning self-defense techniques is a way for good people to do something for themselves and for the good of those with whom they live.

Some Myths about Rape

For a woman, the thought of an attack resulting in the act of rape is so abhorrent that she can hardly bring herself to think of it. Not only must a victim of this vicious attack bear the hardship of the crime itself, but she must also bear the stigma that is attached to the rape act. Believe it or not, there are actually people who believe that women encourage rape acts against them by their behavior or by making themselves available to the crime.

Let's look at some of the most common myths that surround this violent crime.

Since the woman sets the standard for sexual conduct, she could have stopped the rape if she really wanted to.
First of all, rape is not a *sexual* act; rather it is a *violent* act filled with hatred and malice. And even if it were a sexual act, why does the

control of the behavior belong to the woman and not the man? Finally, without defense knowledge and practical skills, the average woman is usually unable to stop the average man in an attack situation, particularly if he is drunk or on drugs.

The woman probably asked for it by the way she dressed.
Rape is now known to be a crime of violence and not a crime of desire or passion; therefore the woman's attire is not even an issue. Even if dress were an issue, no man is *obligated* to rape a seductively dressed woman.

If women would stay at home, they wouldn't get raped.
According to a Denver study of violent crimes, one half of the reported rapes in this country occurred in the home of the victim. This is hardly comforting to the person who believes staying at home fortresses her against attack. This myth implies that women should not leave the home. It is not a reasonable opinion; a large portion of today's work force is female. Surely women have the right to pursue careers as men do. No one should be required to stay at home because of gender.

Women secretly want to be raped.
This is primarily a male fantasy. Women, in general, want to be wooed and won the way they are in romantic novels, but rape is a brutal act which dehumanizes and leaves women's physical and emotional lives in shambles. The man who makes such a statement is using a defense mechanism to excuse either his thought patterns or his behavior.

You cannot thread a moving needle.
This statement implies that if a woman keeps moving fast enough and long enough, she can avoid a rape. The idea is, "If she didn't keep moving, then she must have wanted to be raped." But the fact is that rape victims are most often beaten into submission, or are so terrified of being killed that rape becomes a trade-off for

staying alive. Unfortunately, as is often reported in newspapers, the woman suffers both rape and a brutal death.

Only women with bad reputations get raped, not nice women.
This myth is so ridiculous it hardly bears mentioning. However, some do believe it, again attempting to make the woman responsible for the attack on her.

If a woman really wanted to, she could talk her way out of a rape attack.
Attempting to talk with someone on drugs or someone who is simply on a sick mission of hatred is hopeless; it's like talking to a wall. At the time of an attack, a rapist could not care less about someone else's needs than he does at that moment. He is determined to be violent. A woman's talk is usually of no interest to him. "If she really wanted to" brings up the old question of her desires and cooperation in the rape. Talking is not a reliable deterrant in attack circumstances.

If rape is inevitable, relax and enjoy it.
This is probably the most ridiculous statement of all. The actual physical penetration by the rapist is so excruciatingly painful for the woman that victims have said they thought the pain itself would kill them. During normal intercourse between two people who love each other, the woman is physically prepared for penetration. The walls of the vaginal area are relaxed and receptive. The opposite is true during rape. When a rape is imminent, fright causes the vaginal muscles to tense and constrict. When penetration occurs nevertheless, the pain is monumental for the woman.

Just recently on national television Bobby Knight, the basketball coach from Indiana, made such a statement relating stress to rape. He said that if rape was going to occur, a person should just relax and enjoy it. This kind of thinking is beyond normal reason.

Relax and enjoy it? Just talk with a victim of rape to realize that this statement comes from an uninformed individual.

Examining these myths reminds us that we have not come too far from Adam's statement in early Genesis, "The woman made me do it." Society must quit blaming the woman for being in the wrong place at the wrong time, or for looking a certain way, or for not stopping the attack, or for somehow inviting a rape. We cannot continue to victimize an innocent party a second time.

Let's clear up some more items of misinformation that are generally accepted by a large segment of society.

Rape is an impulsive act.
Not true. Research analysts estimate that 90 percent of all rapes are planned.

One race commits rape against another race.
Again, the statistics clear up this fallacy. 93 percent of the rape incidents that are reported are within the same race.

You can trust an attacker who says he won't hurt you if you cooperate with him.
This is not true, but a terrified woman wants to believe it is true. She will often allow herself to be tied up. This takes away her natural fighting weapons, her arms and legs, and frees the assaulter to do anything he chooses without inhibition.

A woman is incapable of defending herself.
Many success stories have been reported by women who have responded quickly and fiercely at the onset of the attack. The Denver violent crime studies indicate that successful escapes are accomplished by women who have strong, independent personalities.

Myths and misconceptions will set the stage for failure if we allow them to determine values and attitudes toward one segment of our society. Women must help society to recognize and assign the responsibility of violent attack to the guilty party and to stop blaming the victim. Victims are *not* the cause of violent attacks.

3

Who, What, Where, When, and Why

W E'VE LEARNED WHAT RAPE IS *NOT* BY THROWING OUT THE misconceptions, but there is much more to know. Every rape situation is unique, so there is an infinite number of combinations of who, what, where, when, and why. But research on rape reportings give us some clues about why rapists rape, what types of assault there are, and who is susceptible to rape.

Why Rape?

I suppose there are as many reasons for rape as there are rapists. While generalities may be assumed, the definitive cause in each rape case is difficult to determine. One thing is certain, past misconceptions of the "why" of rape no longer hold true. A woman's manner of dress or behavior does not somehow cause enough arousal in a male to put him beyond control. A woman is victimized a second time by the implication that she provoked the attack. I cannot say often enough that the woman is absolutely *not* the guilty party. The attacker is completely to blame and must bear full responsibility for his behavior. Accurate reporting of who the victims are and where the attacks occurred has refuted the theory that "she was asking for it." The increasing number of rapes within the home and rapes against women in their 80's and very young children cannot be ascribed to the way the victims dressed or behaved.

Sociologists, psychologists, and law enforcement people have been puzzled also because rape has increased right along with sexual freedom. With much free sex, no one should be compelled to rape —if rape is simply sexual release. The old "passion and lust" theories simply do not work anymore.

If we can't pinpoint a cause by turning to the victim, then we have to shift our perspective to the rapist himself. If he is not raping to satisfy sexual needs, why is he raping?

Who Rapes?

We have already established that rape is a *violent* act, not an act of desire or lust. Rape is an act of loathing toward one woman or all women. The means of rape is a matter of finding someone who is weak, maimed, helpless, naive, retarded, terrified, or in any way vulnerable enough so that the act may be perpetrated. Some attacks are random; others are planned. The attack is most successful against someone who is frightened into submission or is beaten until she cannot resist. Many times the attack is vicious and might even be extremely perverted. Because of the behaviors evidenced by rapists during attacks, most studies have concluded that rape is not a sex act at all, but rather an act of power and control over a weak victim.

There have been many in-depth studies compiled on the profile of the rapist. Generally speaking, the rapist is usually someone who cannot relate to women, has mother image problems, and has a low self-esteem regarding his masculinity. If life "fails" him, he blames his mother, his wife, his children, or any other woman he can find to strike out at in anger. Without question, the most violent rape act of all is when a woman is assaulted by more than one person—a gang attack. These are men attempting to prove their masculinity in front of one another. The result is unspeakable violence for the woman.

A rapist will try to absolve himself from the act and blame the woman. He will claim that she is the cause of his actions because she sent him "signals" or because, for some obscure reason of his own, he believes she deserves what she got. There have been cases where the rapist's male ego has so distorted his perception of the rape that he has actually courted his victim from his jail cell.

Strangely enough, most rapists believe child molesters to be "sick" and, if given the opportunity in prison, may try to kill such a person. Often rapists have children of their own, and they find child molesting reprehensible.

Along with the hate factor is the desire and need for the rapist to dominate another human being completely. Not only is the assaulter trying to humiliate and debase his victim, he feels strong and powerful when he has someone terrified and under his command. During the victimization, he believes he gains potency in his own life; therefore, the violence feeds his needs. The degree to which he harms his victim is relative to the power he feels while in control. In some instances, a weapon is used in order to back up his need to feel powerful and masterful over others.

Whether because of hatred, drug abuse, or heavy drinking, the attacker cannot be counted on to be merciful in any way. If he is suffering from a macho image and is urged to demonstrate his prowess in front of others, his brutality might know no boundaries. An attacker could also be insane, disturbed, or so perverted in his lifestyle that his behavior is a type of weird performance.

What about Attacks and Attackers?

There are many kinds of violent assaults. They range from verbal harassment to brutality and death. There is a great temptation to ignore or reject the existence of such inhumane acts. In order to deal with the problem of assault effectively, we must acknowledge the reality and possibility of assault at any time and go on from there.

Besides female rape there are many types of attacks. We'll look at some of the most commonly reported methods used by attackers.

Peeping Toms
Peeping Toms are most often considered harmless because their method of activity is somewhat private. However, one day simple "peeping" may not be as thrilling or powerful as it once was, so the peeper's dysfunctional attitudes might take other devious paths.

Definitely do your best to remember the physical characteristics of a peeper and report his behavior to the police.

Exhibitionism
Exhibitionists, like the "peepers," are nearly always men and are considered to be physically harmless during the act of exhibiting. The thrill of shocking a woman to screams or tears is exhilarating and forms the incentive for their behavior.

The most effective reaction is for a woman to display calmness and to make a remark that deflates the exhibitionist's ego. By being stoic and providing no hysterical response, she takes the control of an ugly situation away from the offender.

Homosexual rape

Homosexual rape occurs most often in prisons by both males and females. Until recently, our society has avoided talking about it. Of women raped by men, approximately one out of ten reports the rape. The male rape reporting factor is many, many times less, almost to an unknown point. Why this difference? The male reasoning for not reporting a rape is that many men could not bear the humiliation of having their masculinity questioned. This differs greatly from a woman's feelings after she has been raped. Her femininity is not called into question.

Child molesting

The child molester is very dangerous. He preys on unsuspecting children who trust him. The harm from this act, especially if it is a continuing one, is so destructive that the personality of the child can be troubled through adulthood. More than likely, a normal sex life will be difficult or even impossible. Young males who have been molested often become molesters themselves in later life.

Incest

Incest is usually a father, stepfather, or another male member of the household having sexual relations with young girls and/or boys in the family. Until recently, this was almost unheard of as a problem in this country. Now that some of the stigma has been lifted, scores of appalling stories are being told of sexual and physical abuse by family members toward their children. The child is particularly vulnerable to sexual abuse because so much trust is placed in adults. An adult is able to manipulate a trusting young mind into the acceptability of a physical relationship without the child realizing what is happening to him or her. When the child relates the occurrences to the mother, the incidents are often ignored or the child is accused of lying. Even though a spouse may be suspicious of questionable behavior by the mate toward the child, the fears are set aside for fear of disgrace or retaliation. So the incest continues, and the child is driven into further confusion and abuse.

Such abuses will not stop without firm intervention. A child does not have the resources to fight against such overwhelming circumstances.

Spouse battering

Although there are cases of women who physically abuse their husbands, the large portion of batterings are inflicted by men who abuse their wives. Some disoriented men have considered beating their wives a part of their marriage privileges. Police departments and local authorities have avoided involvement in matrimonial problems, including battering. Because of this lack of support by law enforcement agencies, women have very little protection. If two men fought on the street, one could be charged with assault and battery. But in a marriage relationship, women have had to endure beatings with little recourse for help.

Many women continue to be battered, broken, and some have died for lack of attention to their pleas. But this situation has improved dramatically! Today there are crisis clinics and hotlines for battered women seeking help. But resolutions continue to be difficult because the battered women fear retaliatory beatings and even death for themselves and their children.

Date/acquaintance rape

One of the most difficult attacks to understand and define is rape by someone who is fairly well known to the victim. It is also the most under-reported type of rape. When two people come to a sexual crossroads, with one party saying "yes" and the other saying "no," it is still called "rape" if one person forces the other. It does not matter that it is a friend, relative, neighbor, co-worker, or social acquaintance. It cannot be called a "seduction," a "mistake," or "payment for an entertaining evening." It is *rape*.

In the case of date/acquaintance rape, the problem of identifying what actually happened is increased for the victim. She seeks to understand what she did to make him think he could get away with such an act. She often blames herself, assumes the guilt, and lives in the "If only I had not . . ." world. The woman must remember that a person who commits such an act does not believe himself to be at fault. Usually he honestly believes that the woman wanted and expected him to behave the way he did. After all, that is how the movies sometimes portray women, saying "no" to begin with and finally swooning as the man proceeds despite her protests. The movies don't tell the agony and viciousness of the attack for the victim. The man who treats women in such a manner feeds his ego and fantasizes about his ability to conquer women.

Some startling facts were discovered in a recent study on date rape. Seven thousand students at thirty-five colleges and universities across the country were interviewed in this study financed by the National Institute of Mental Health. One woman student in eight had been raped, according to the legal definition of rape, in the year previous to the survey. 90 percent of the women knew their attackers, and more than 90 percent of the women did not report the rape. Other studies at universities have turned up similar statistics. Date rape is much more common than we'd like to believe!

Who Are the Victims?

Who is susceptible to sexual attack? Unfortunately, the answer to this question is *everyone*. Certainly all women, young and old, are susceptible, and many males as well. According to reports, males are being subjected to attack by other males more than ever before. There is also an increasing number of rapes reported by grandmothers, disabled women, and children of all ages. Even babies have been assaulted. This new information regarding assault against women and children is not only shocking, but it has radically altered social and psychological conclusions regarding victim selection. It has destroyed the notion that attacks occur because the attacker seeks sexual gratification.

There was a time when people felt safe in their homes or in suburban and rural communities. Today that feeling is a false security. Sexual attacks occur in large and small cities, on farms and estates, on the street and in the home. There is nowhere in the world where you are totally free from the possibility of attack. In many countries, rape is a common part of life.

Many unsuspecting women have become victims of rape because of this false sense of security. An intelligent attacker can easily enter a home by the permission of a gullible person. In the guise of a repairman for the phone, electricity, or plumbing, an appropriately dressed criminal gets into an apartment or home without any difficulty. Of the thirteen tragic killings of women by the Boston strangler, twelve of the women allowed the killer to gain entrance into their residences because he used this approach.

There is a large segment of the female population which is vulnerable to attack simply because, either by nature or profession, they desire to help someone in distress. The assailant sometimes fakes an injury to get a woman to stop and help him. Social workers, medical professionals, teachers, and others trained to assist needy people often become the victims while trying to help. Not only is the potential victim physically vulnerable in that moment of aid, she is also viewed by the attacker as someone who can be duped and manipulated.

You probably remember the well-publicized case of Ted Bundy, who brutally raped and murdered a great number of young women (he claims to have lost count somewhere around one hundred). Bundy would park his car in an out-of-the-way place on a college or university campus at night. After putting his arm in a sling, he'd carry an armload of books. When he spotted a potential victim, he'd conveniently drop the books near her and struggle with his "hurt" arm to pick them up. Usually the girl offered to take his books to his car. Bundy played on a natural response to help a needy person.

It's too easy to forget or ignore the statistics, or feel that rape is a problem you will never be involved with. Don't think, "It could never happen to me." *It could*. Train your mind to be alert to times and places that are potential danger spots, knowing that an attack is a possibility.

How It Happens

Again, each rape incident is as unique as each rapist—and each victim. But there are a few general ways a rapist interacts with a victim, and there is a certain progression to an attack.

Physical assaults against women are often planned in advance. The assaulter spends time thinking about what he is going to do. More than likely it will be only hours or minutes before the actual attack, not days. For example, during a home invasion for burglary purposes, the perpetrator does not wish to encounter anyone, but his backup plan is assault or rape if he does happen to find a woman at home.

The Five Stages of an Attack

According to police reports an attack usually has five phases that follow a distinct pattern.

The first stage of an attack is usually *surveillance*. Surveillance can take place in a supermarket, shopping mall, or any public place. The attacker has no particular pattern for choosing a victim. He might determine to assault the next person who walks through a doorway. If you walked through his selected doorway, he would probably follow you to an isolated place such as your home, your work place, or your car. Without becoming paranoid, you should always be aware of strangers around you.

The second step in an attack is usually *verbal contact*. In order to test a victim's resistance, the attacker initiates contact with a comment. If you are confronted with such a situation, do your best not to demonstrate timidity or vulnerability in any way, or he will certainly proceed with his plans. He wants to dominate. He considers himself a sort of hunter, and the victim is the hunted.

Another form of verbal contact is a sexual suggestion or innuendo. If you respond with embarrassment or shock, you immediately indicate that you are unprepared to deal with a crisis. This is a pivotal point in the encounter. Try to make a decisive, firm comment to get rid of him. Your comment could be a clear indication of your unquestionable rejection of any further contact on his part.

Physical contact is usually the third stage of an attack. Physical contact takes two forms. The first takes place in public. An attacker brushes up against you in the supermarket to test your timidity. He quickly picks up signs of vulnerability by your reactions. Test yourself. The next time you are bumped, see if you back off with profuse apologies or if you hold your ground.

Another form of physical contact is more serious. The attacker might grab you to pull you away. The best response is to lash out immediately with a powerful blow. This is when successful self defense begins. If you fight with great force and vigor, you might bombard the invader/attacker into letting you go. Since most assaulters choose a victim they expect to conquer, yours won't be too happy to discover he has a wild and crazy woman on his hands.

Stage four is the *actual rape*. If you are attacked, try to stay on your feet as long as possible. But even if you have battled your way down to the ground, there is still time to resist forcefully and escape. Remember the powerful name of Jesus, and fight with any arm, leg, finger, or toe that you have free. If the attacker holds your arms, use your knees, legs, and feet. If he's got your legs, use your elbows, forearms, and fists. If you're completely pinned, use your head to butt the attacker's face and your mouth to bite everything in reach.

The last part of an attack is called *termination*. If the assault gets this far, be very quiet, stoic, and demonstrate no fear. Don't threaten to retaliate or report him to the authorities. You could cause the attacker to panic. A panicked attacker could kill his victim to keep her quiet.

It's disturbing to think that someone could be watching you and planning an attack. Unfortunately, it is a real possibility. But the crucial question is, *How swiftly can you respond in a potentially dangerous episode?* You won't be able to respond quickly unless you make some clear, definite decisions regarding resistance to attack prior to an assault.

There is a wide range of possible behaviors that could take place within this five-stage structure of a rape episode. It is nearly impossible to predict a pattern of behavior for the rapist. But we'll talk about a few common methods attackers use to dominate a victim.

The first is *verbal intimidation*. Verbal threats of brutality and death will often be quite enough to force a woman to cooperate. Many victims have yielded to rape out of terror at the attacker's mention of a knife in a pocket. They didn't need to see that knife; their fear was real enough.

Another method of rape coercion is *threat with a weapon*. Reports vary regarding the percentage of attacks involving a weapon. When faced with a gun or knife, the victim should try not to panic. If possible, try to convince the attacker that he does not need the gun. If at any time the gun is set aside, you will have gained a better opportunity to escape.

A third method is *threat of retaliation*. An attacker may threaten to harm you again or someone else in your family if you report him. When an assaulter molests children, he sometimes uses the threat of killing family members if the child tells anyone what has happened. An assaulter may threaten an adult victim with humiliation and lies that would make it seem as though the victim had initiated the encounter.

Finally, remember our discussion about an assaulter's *use of pity*. Women who desire to please and help others often become victims of attack when they stop to meet a need. The Christian woman especially feels guilty, as though she is not living for Christ or being a good Samaritan if she does not stop to help a stranger. Attackers count on this response. If the situation warrants your attention and there are many people around, it may be safe to go ahead, but be careful!

When It's Over

A rape attack is so traumatic and terrifying that it leaves a lifelong mark on the victim. She never forgets the experience, and, according to reports by victims, the rape shapes her view of herself, her family, her friends, and her life. Only another rape victim knows the horror and humiliation of begging and pleading for her life to be spared.

Rape victims commonly experience these reactions in varying degrees: depression, fear, deep anxiety, loss of self-esteem, loss of relationships with family and friends, loss of the ability to function in normal activities, and an inability to relate sexually to the opposite sex.

Time for physical healing must follow a rape because of the damage done to the victim's body. I mentioned before that the physically violent rape act is excruciating to women. Because the woman is terrified, the vaginal muscle contracts and becomes inelastic instead of relaxed and receptive. So the small, constricted area is torn when a violent penetration occurs. Sometimes the muscles tear into the rectal area. Penetration of a child is even more painful because of the small vaginal opening.

Another medical consideration is that the victim could become pregnant during the rape act. Wisdom, support, legal and psychological counseling, and physical care are critical at this stage.

If the victim of rape is a married woman, difficulties in her relationship with her husband can be part of the aftermath of rape. The relationship often becomes strained, resulting in separation. Of rape assault victims who are married, more than 50 percent are separated or divorced within a year after the attack. The emotional strain on both of the marriage partners creates stress to a breaking point. Physical contact is tense because the woman's view of intercourse has been damaged as well as her view of herself. The victim often feels unworthy and terrified of intimacy. Occasionally the husband experiences doubts about whether the attack could have been prevented or not. Doubt and uncertainty displayed by the partner creates a "last-straw" syndrome for the victim who desperately needs to reestablish her validity as a human being. More than ever before, she needs to be treated with love and patience. The situation requires superhuman understanding on the part of both parties in order to restore the relationship. Christian couples can appropriate God's grace and power to heal in this difficult situation. Christian counseling for both husband and wife is helpful; both need direction and support.

We can never fully measure the emotional and psychological damage to the rape victim. Shame, self-rejection, and self-degradation are so overwhelming that the rape victim cannot recover without a great deal of support. Even more important than counseling is the support of family and friends who will participate with the victim in the stages of recovery.

A recurring sense of guilt is another common reaction. The victim will often unreasonably perceive herself to be at fault for not preventing the attack.

Fear is another prevailing emotion for the assault victim. She remembers the attack and fears the places, people, and things that surround her. Every shadow and doorway hides a potential attacker. God can provide freedom from this inhibiting emotion. 2 Timothy 1:17 promises a spirit of power and love to replace a spirit of fear. Trust God. Commit the past, present, and future into his able hands.

You now have overwhelming amounts of information about rape —who, what, where, when, and why. Are you feeling a bit helpless in the face of all these statistics and possible attack situations? Don't let fear get a hold on you! We have a powerful God who loves us, and we have able minds and bodies to apply to the problem of assault.

4

A Place to Begin

W E'VE DISCOVERED THAT GOD VALUES WOMEN AND we've cleared up some misconceptions about women and about rape. We've also talked about rape, rapists, victims, and the aftermath of rape. All that information adequately covers the problem —now let's talk about the solution!

Most Christian women don't naturally develop a philosophy of self defense. They don't learn to fight or to defend themselves at home, at school, or at Sunday school. But it is important that women think through and develop a concept of self defense. This chapter should help.

The Christian's Secret Weapons

God is omnipresent—he is in all places, at all times. He has promised Christians that they will never be forsaken or alone. The

Bible says that God goes before us, behind us, and places his hand of blessing on our heads (Psalm 139:5, TLB). While Christians are not spared troubles or disasters, they are guided by their belief in a Supreme Being who has everything in control and is ever present with them.

God gives _angels_ charge over Christians as well, not to save them from problems but to be present in times of need (Psalm 91). Over the years, amazing stories have been reported about the appearance of "beings" in crisis situations. Many who have witnessed superhuman interventions believe these are angels sent directly by God.

In the book _Angels_, Billy Graham tells the story of a missionary family threatened by a whole tribe of natives in another country. The little group huddled in their small home, praying for God's protection while hundreds of angry tribesmen stood outside. At the end of that long day, the natives simply disassembled and left the area. The family was amazed! Years later, one of the nationals who had been in that mob became a Christian. The missionaries asked him why the tribe had not attacked the family that day. His response was incredible. He said the natives retreated because they were afraid of all the people in white uniforms standing guard around the house! Surely they were angels.

A student related an event that took place on a midwestern university campus. One evening she needed to get from one part of campus to another. Since she was in a hurry, she took a shortcut through a secluded area which students had been warned to avoid. As she passed through the alley, she noticed a man leaning against a wall. Praying fervently for God's protection, she quickly passed through the alley without incident. Shortly after she returned to her room, she heard that a rape had occurred in the same alley just after she had gone through the area. Believing that she could help identify the attacker who had been apprehended, she went directly to the police. She recognized the man from the alley and was permitted to speak to him. "Why didn't you attack me when I walked through earlier?" He responded that it would have been foolish, since she had those two large men walking on either side of her. You can bet that young woman believes in the existence of angels!

There have been many reportings of angel intervention by Christians who have had lifesaving experiences. I encourage you to read Corrie ten Boom's books on angel protection during her concentration camp days. I also recommend Betty Maltz's book, *Angels Watching Over Us* (Old Tappan, NJ: Fleming H. Revell, 1986), and *When Angels Appear* by Hope MacDonald (Grand Rapids, MI: Zondervan, 1982).

According to Scripture, it is the *Holy Spirit* who gives the believer wisdom, insight, direction, and a source of inner power. When the Spirit resides within you, your physical body has become the temple of God. So a rape assault against you would be an assault on God's temple. The child of God has the right to call on the Holy Spirit for help in difficult times—particularly in attack situations.

The disciples of the New Testament church and others discovered that there was power in the verbal use of *the name of Jesus Christ*. A study of the New Testament reveals countless uses of the phrase, "in the name of Jesus." In Christ's name the blind have been made to see, the lame to walk, and demons cast out of possessed people. Perhaps we modern-day Christians do not realize the potential power in appropriating the name of Christ. John 14:14 states, "For if you ask anything in my name . . ." Belief is the method, and prayer is the means.

A local newspaper told the story of a missionary lady who was accosted by an assaulter while here in the United States on furlough. She quickly called on God, crying out, "Jesus, help me!" The startled assaulter asked her what she had said. She repeated the words, "Jesus, help me." Immediately, the attacker released her, turned, and fled. Her main line of self defense was the name of Christ.

After much thought, evaluation, discussion, and reading, I have concluded that the name of Jesus Christ holds enormous power today, just as it did in New Testament days. If there is power in the name of Jesus (and the Bible says there is) and if Christians have the right to call on him (and the Bible says they do), then why not call on that wonderful name for protection in violent situations? We can, and we should.

Personal Equipment for Self Defense

I mentioned earlier that self worth and determination in attack go hand in hand. *Self worth* also takes on new meaning when you come into a personal relationship with an all-powerful, all-knowing, all-loving God. As Christian people, we are created by him, indwelt by his Holy Spirit, united with his Son, and cherished and protected by his angels. We are worthy in our own right as children of the King!

Recognition of self worth is followed by a *resolve to fight for what is right*. There comes a deep, inner resolve to resist anything that tries to destroy that which you hold dear—the life God has given you. You can learn to fight for yourself in the way you would fight if someone were trying to harm your best friend or a member of your family.

In an old movie, Barbara Stanwyck delivers a priceless line. Aboard a ship, she struggles with a villain who tries to throw her overboard. They wrestle, and the attacker goes overboard instead. Later she tells the story to a friend, "I knew that one of us was going overboard, and in my mind, it narrowed down to him." That's great resolve!

Another powerful asset is *knowledge of pain points*. We'll talk about pain points later in greater detail. For now, realize that everybody has several areas on their body where pain is easily inflicted. All you need is one good blow to gain time to escape.

Adrenalin is another great weapon in the arsenal of self defense. In any stressful circumstance or situation where fear, anger, hatred, and other extreme emotions are aroused, the body releases a surge of adrenalin into the physical system which increases body strength to enormous proportions. The parasympathetic nervous system is activated to such a point that people have been known to perform incredible feats of strength well beyond known abilities. Have you ever read stories of a parent literally lifting a car off a trapped child, or of a small person carrying a heavy person out of a burning building, or of people running faster than humanly possible in an emergency? This superhuman "fight or flight" system is the great equalizer, and when utilized properly, adrenalin is a great factor in successful defense escapes.

In an attack event, there is usually a momentary fear which is temporarily paralyzing. That is the moment when the adrenalin is pouring through your body and everything seems to freeze. The amount of adrenalin seems to be proportional to the amount of fear. Picture this mentally: Imagine adrenalin pouring into your body; you are physically more powerful than you have ever been. Imagine an attacker coming up to you while you have all that power. All you need to know now is where to strike to send that universal message of pain.

Gathering together all that we know—that we are worthy of defense, that we can resolve to defend, that we have the right and responsibility to defend, and that we have human and super-human resources for defense—we are now ready to move on to the nitty-gritty particulars of self defense.

5

It's All in Your Head

S ELF DEFENSE BEGINS IN YOUR MIND —IN BEING MENTALLY prepared and being savvy about potentially dangerous situations. You can anticipate your determination to protect yourself, and you can become knowledgeable about attack possibilities.

Mental Preparation

I just claimed that self defense begins in your mind. Have you determined in your mind that you are going to fight back forcefully if attacked? That determination is your best preparation. Inventory the value you place on yourself and determine the degree to which you would resist in order to save yourself from attack.

People with low self-esteem and those who are terrified of pain and death are most likely to be unsuccessful in resisting attack. Studies have shown that a woman who resists quickly and with great force is far more likely to escape than a woman who hesitates and is unsure. These same studies report that most of the women who have escaped have very strong personalities and feel good about who they are.

If you are naturally timid, spend some time considering your right before God and society to take care of yourself. You are God's creation and have the right to live free from violent attack. Picture yourself in an attack situation. Do you see yourself responding with vigor? Perhaps at this point you are unsure of your response because you lack the physical defense skills. Don't think about what you don't know, but try to visualize yourself responding with what every person knows —biting, kicking, and scratching.

If you cannot materialize this picture, then visualize a stranger trying to harm your child, your sister, or your mother. How do you react in this imagined scenario? Let your feelings come forward in your imagination. Are you angry that someone wants to hurt your child or other loved ones? Would you hesitate to defend yourself but respond immediately for your loved one? If so, why is there a difference? Do you honor yourself as God's creation? If not, why not?

These questions are extremely significant. You will fight quickly for that which you honor, and you will hesitate or not respond at all for that which you hold in low esteem. Check out your self-value with friends. Regardless of your self estimation, God placed the highest rating on your worthiness. Value yourself as he values you—with love.

Here are a few general principles of self defense to help you develop a response mentality. Review them until they are firmly imbedded in your mind.

Fighting dirty is fair

Once you've learned some self-defense techniques well, be prepared to use them to the limit. There are no rules and no referees. There are no holds barred—no injury is too severe when brutalization, rape, or murder is a possibility. Self defense is every person for himself or herself. This might sound terrible to you, but self defense is simply dirty street fighting in every imaginable form. Any and every tactic can be used, whether it seems fair or "dirty." You're fighting for space and time to escape, no matter what it takes.

Never say never

Don't set physical limitations on yourself by saying, "But I could never do that!" The law of survival in your spirit is strong. And that adrenalin-powered self-defense mechanism inside you is triggered into action when you are attacked. It is amazing what a determined woman with a committed mind can do!

Practice makes permanent

When you learn a new skill, it's best to practice detailed actions with slow, deliberate movements. Stop between movements and analyze what you are doing; you don't want to practice errors. Accuracy comes first; speed comes later.

Once you've mastered the techniques, practice them faithfully. Like anything new, these skills will not come instinctively in an emergency situation. They say a new skill must be practiced a thousand times before you can respond on an unconscious level. Work with a partner or with a group of people—you will all improve your skills.

Keep it to yourself

Don't announce to everyone that you are practicing self-defense skills. It will take a while to develop those skills, and some friend might teasingly challenge you to demonstrate your expertise before you know what you are doing. The attack scenario cannot be accurately constructed in play or practice. First, your skills will be limited at first, although hopefully you will be ready should a real attack situation come up. Second, your friend expects a response; in a real attack your assailant will not. And because you are not truly surprised or afraid, your system has not released adrenalin. Your true ability at self defense cannot be proven with someone you know. A great deal of your success is derived from the element of surprise, from the power which comes from fear-induced adrenalin. Of course, you cannot truly injure your friend, while in a real attack you would inflict as serious an injury as you can deliver. That's hardly a good way to prove your abilities to a friend! So don't subject yourself to friends who want to test you.

Believe in yourself
Believe in your potential for defense. Resolve comes first, then technique, and then freedom. Thomas Dryden said, "They can conquer who believe they can." Keep reminding yourself that you will be successful.

The assault continues until either you or your attacker wins. Determine in your mind (like Barbara Stanwyck who tossed her movie-assailant overboard) that you will be the winner. Rehearse in your mind the picture of rejecting defeat in an attack situation.

Believe in self defense
Believe in your responsibility to defend yourself for your own sake and for the sake of your family and society. If an attacker is successful with you, his next victim could be your friend or neighbor. Who will stop him if you don't? You have to hurt him to keep him from hurting you and others.

Part of being mentally prepared is having considered the possibilities and having thought through your responses. A woman who has never even thought about being attacked will be so surprised that she'll have to stop and think about what to do. You don't have time for that! Think about some of these danger spots now.

Telephone Troubles

Many times the telephone is used to bother you or as part of an attacker's or burglar's "surveillance." It is important for you to settle on a "phone philosophy," a policy of responding to calls only on your own terms.

Nuisance callers
Some callers are persistent with obscene or irritating calls just to be a nuisance. Usually these callers are dialing at random. Don't be afraid of such calls. You have various options for handling these repeat callers. One way is to hang up immediately without engaging in conversation at all. You might try blowing a loud, metal whistle into the receiver. Another technique is to listen, then say, "Operator, this is the call I want traced." That small deception is often enough to get rid of a persistent nuisance.

If serious types of calls continue, you can place a tracer on your phone in cooperation with the police department and the telephone company.

Surveillance callers
A more dangerous caller is the one who elicits information about your lifestyle to determine your "at home" patterns in order to harm you or burglarize your home. Unless you have considered the possibility that you are a potential victim, it is easy to drop clues or information without ever being aware of it.

As a general rule, women who live by themselves should not list their feminine names in the phone book. A single female listing such as, "Smith, Mary" is a dead giveaway that no males reside in the home. You might list your name as, "Smith, M.J." or even create a phantom roommate and list, "Smith, M.J. and T.J." As an experiment, check a single page of your local phone book to note how many women have unwittingly informed the public that they live alone.

When someone incorrectly dials your phone number and you want to be helpful, say, "No one is here by that name," and ask, "What number did you want?" If the number is incorrect, tell the caller, but do *not* offer your number as well. If the caller had the right number but the wrong name, be careful not to divulge too much information. Don't say, "No, I'm here all by myself." Or, "There's no *Bob* here, just Nancy and Peggy." An answer of, "Right number, wrong person" is all that is necessary.

Don't respond to callers who seek information about your name, age, or the number of people residing at your address. Instruct your babysitters never to give out information but only to take messages.

Never tell a stranger in an unsolicited phone call whether you will or will not be home at a specific time.

There are even criminals who call a home to inform the owners that they have won a prize. They give detailed directions for when and where the prize is to be claimed. When the "prize-winners" leave their home to claim their prize, the caller goes in to rob the house. To determine the legitimacy of such a call, get personal and company information regarding the caller, then call for verification. If the information checks out, there should be no specified time for you to leave your home to claim a prize.

We all want to be considered polite, helpful people. But unfortunately, many criminals rely on our naive responses to unsolicited calls. One common query is, "May I speak to the man of the house?" An openly truthful response such as, "No, he died years ago; I'm a widow" or "He's at work right now" can supply information to a stranger who has no business knowing anything about you.

The significant point is to protect yourself and your home from criminals who use the telephone to gain information. It is your phone and your household; you are *not* being rude when you choose not to respond to questions, but only wise and prudent. It is not "rude" or "unChristian" to use good judgment.

Home and Apartment Invasion

Normally, it would be safe to assume that we are secure in our own homes and apartments. That's an assumption we can no longer afford. As I said earlier, the highest percentage of rapes and attacks against women occur in the place of residence. Let's look at some ways to safeguard your home from potential attacks, as well as some general techniques to look out for.

Some safeguards
Although this may seem paranoid, if you are looking for a house to buy and you live alone, don't buy one on a corner lot. According to police reports, corner houses are burglarized most often because there are more directions for the burglar's getaway, and fewer neighbors to observe criminal activity. The same idea holds true for apartments. Middle apartments are safer than isolated units. While you might desire more privacy, first floor, top floor, and end units are more prone to plunder.

Think about installing outside lights to illuminate your yard. These should be secured high enough to prevent easy tampering. Flood lights in dark areas, although accessible to burglars, are a good deterrent.

Your mailbox should never indicate that you live alone. The mailbox could read like the phone book with initials only or a phantom roommate. Never list your first name on the box.

Entrance doors should have no glass in them. Peepholes in a solid door are better.

The lock on your door is only as good as the strength of the door jamb. Examine your door frame to see if it could withstand a solid kick. Install a deadbolt lock that is at least one inch in length on every entrance door. Chain locks on doors are easily maneuvered by the average burglar. If you come home and find an entrance door open, do not go inside, or you may be trapped with a panicked burglar. Go directly to a neighbor's house and call the police.

Your windows should have a keylocked system or nails placed in holes in corners.

If you have an electric door system in the garage, be aware that some thieves use electric frequency scanners which easily open those doors. Flip off the power switch to the garage-door opening unit at night and during long periods of absence from your home.

Avoid leaving keys anywhere outside the house. They are easily found by the novice burglar.

If you live in an apartment, always use lighted stairways and entrances. If a stranger is lingering in your hallway, do not go into your apartment. Leave, or knock on a neighbor's door.

It is difficult for the average person to be knowledgeable regarding the value and effectiveness of alarm systems because there are so many. Commercial organizations don't help because they want only to sell their product. Don't waste thousands of dollars on a useless system. Check with your local police department and consumer's research organizations for recommended alarm systems.

Keep them out!

Attackers or burglars have a multitude of creative techniques for getting into your home. We talked about some of these when we covered telephone abusers.

Another common ruse for gaining entrance to your home is the offer of free household products in return for responses to a survey. If you answer the questions on the survey, examine the form to determine whether a criminal could use the information to establish a profile regarding your household activities. Size of the household, income, value of the house, type of car, hobbies, investment information—all of these tell a great deal about your lifestyle and household pattern. Those free household products are not worth risking burglary.

Be aware of the timeworn ruse of gaining entrance into an apartment by the statement, "The landlord sent me." Once the impostor is inside, everyone is vulnerable. A legitimate repairman won't mind waiting in the hallway while you confirm his request with the landlord. And so what if he does?! Don't you value your life and home more than his inconvenience? Don't be deceived by a badge or a uniform and allow entrance to a person who has no right to be in your home.

Going Up?

An elevator is another potential danger spot. Because it isolates you with an attacker for a brief or extended period of time, you are vulnerable to all kinds of attacks.

The attacker is counting on your preoccupation with thoughts of where you are going so that you don't pay attention to him. If there are only two of you waiting to enter an elevator, wait for the next one. Attackers have been known to hang around an elevator waiting for a single woman to step inside. He might slip into the elevator just before the door closes. I have heard many stories of robbery and physical violence which took place in elevator encounters.

If you are uncomfortable in an elevator situation, go immediately to the control panel and place your hand directly next to the alarm button. If you feel safe enough, continue to your floor, but you may want to get off at the next floor. With your hand at the control panel, keep your eyes on the suspected person. If he makes any movement toward you, press the alarm. Make a habit of standing near the control panel every time you ride an elevator. Usually no one will notice your habit; they normally don't care where you stand or what you do.

Regardless of what did or did not occur between the two of you in an uneasy elevator situation, be the last one to leave the elevator. If you go first, your back is to the stranger, leaving you vulnerable to attack. Don't worry about offending someone who wants to be polite and let you exit first. It doesn't matter what that stranger will think of you.

Riding an elevator seems harmless enough, so you may not have ever considered your vulnerability. But if you are serious about learning to avoid attack, you need to change your patterns of thinking about and responding to your surroundings. Without becoming paranoid, look around and identify potentially dangerous places that you have never thought about before. Remember, killers and rapists are not necessarily big, ugly people. Ted Bundy, that notorious women-killer, is handsome with an engaging and sociable personality. But he is not someone with whom you would choose to be alone in an elevator.

Public Transportation

There was a time when people could be safe in public just by being in the presence of other people. You could expect to be safe from attack if you were in a crowd. Unfortunately, today this is not true. Victims have related countless stories of vicious attack in the presence or within earshot of bystanders. Waiting for and riding on public transportation vehicles have their own peculiar pitfalls.

Stay as close to the front of a bus as possible, even if it means standing. Some have advocated sitting at the middle of the bus, where escape through the side door is easiest. However, you could end up in an unfamiliar neighborhood more dangerous than the bus. And if the bus leaves, you are in even more trouble than before!

Standing at a bus stop or waiting on a train platform in a big city is not time for making social acquaintances. Stay in the middle of a group, away from secluded areas.

Here's some more general, good advice. Even though it is humiliating and insulting, most police authorities recommend that you give up your valuables and money if they are demanded. Better to be robbed than killed!

Car Invasion

Women are often abducted or assaulted in or near their own cars or the cars of their assailants. Women have disappeared while walking to their cars in shopping mall parking lots or at their places of work. Assailants will hang out in the parking lot to survey and plan the abduction of a child or a woman.

When you are leaving from any place, get your car key out and ready just before you leave the premises. This prevents your having to fumble for the key by the side of the car.

There are several gimmicks to get an unsuspecting person into a car. Attackers will often follow a woman to her car. Then, just as she is bending down to put her packages away, the criminal will force her into the car by threat of a weapon and then get into the car beside her. So look around before you get into your car. Check the back seat. Put your packages into the car and look around again. Then immediately get into the car. Lock yourself in— something we all forget to do. When away from our cars, we lock others out to protect *the car*. But we often neglect to protect a more valuable commodity— *ourselves*! It should become a habit, night and day.

A story appeared in the newspaper relating a rather frightening story. A woman pulled into a gas station. After the attendant filled her car with gas, he engaged the woman in an argument regarding payment for the gas. Finally, he demanded that she step inside the station to sort out the problem. After she got inside, the attendant informed her that there was a man crouched on the floor of her car behind the driver's seat. She should have checked her backseat, whether or not her car was locked.

Remember the story of Ted Bundy? His ruse was to fake an injury or make a false request for information and help. Helpful women fell into the trap. This is also a common approach. If this happens to you in a parking lot of a store, keep your distance and head directly back to the store for help. If the stranger's need is legitimate, a store employee can help. If it is not, the person will be gone before you return.

Even traveling in a moving car can present problems. Place your purse under the seat out of sight. There are purse grabbers who smash windows. If you're driving in a questionable area, stay in the inside lane, away from possible curbside approaches.

Not too long ago I had an experience which might have been disastrous except for the grace of God. On my way to a basketball game in Chicago, I took a wrong turn and ended up directly in the heart of the most dangerous part of the city. The night was dark, and every turn I made took me deeper into unknown territory. Buildings were torn down, garbage littered the streets, and teenagers were milling around in groups. It was a single woman's nightmare, and I was terrified! In desperation, I cried aloud, "Jesus, help me!" Right at that moment I made a left turn. Immediately a siren sounded, and I was pulled over by the police. That was one time I was _glad_ to hear that siren behind my car! Not only was it the police, it was two wonderful women police officers; they told me I had no business being where I was alone. It turned out that I was forty blocks from my destination. The officers instructed me to look straight ahead, and they would follow me for twenty blocks. They followed me with a spotlight shining directly into my car. Once I'd passed the twentieth block I was in safe territory, and the officers waved goodbye to me. If I hadn't already believed in miracles, I would have then! Who would have thought a prayer could be answered by an illegal left turn?

If you are approached by an obviously malicious person, lay on the horn and don't stop until the person leaves. If you can see that the attacker is about to enter your car, push in your cigarette lighter and keep your hand on the knob ready to use it when a hand comes in the window. Check out your car now to see if any parts (turnsignal, gearshift lever) unscrew to use as weapons. I carry a flashlight with a loud siren. It is better to have something like that than to wish that you did!

If you notice that you are being followed by another car, don't drive directly home and run into the house. You will have informed a potential assaulter of your place of residence. Instead, drive to a gas station or, better yet, to a police or fire station.

People are also sometimes assaulted and robbed when their cars break down by the roadside. If you are in a busy area, raise your hood, get inside the car, and lock the doors. Don't roll down your windows or respond to anyone who wants to help unless the person's car has a family in it. There are actually people who drive around looking for women with car trouble. Once a man fixed a flat tire for a woman and then raped her. Who can understand that kind of "helpful" mentality? Make or buy a sign that says, "Send help" to place in the rear window of your car. Always keep it in your car.

If your car breaks down in a deserted area, it is sometimes best to raise the hood and get completely away from the car out of sight. Stay there until a state patrolman comes along, or a man with a family in the car drives up. Be cautious of accepting help from truck drivers. The majority are wonderful and helpful, but there have been cases of truck drivers assaulting women.

If you find yourself in the car with a criminal who says he will kill you if you don't do as he says, you have to make some choices.

If he makes you drive to an isolated area, it is likely that he plans to kill you anyway. If you believe he plans to kill you, resist the attack right away. If you are driving, you could wreck the car at a very low speed, especially on his side of the car. If he is driving with both hands on the wheel, then claw his face and eyes and risk the wreck. It is a hard choice, but sometimes a passive victim makes the aggressor feel more powerful and, ultimately, more brutal.

Other than these personal precautionary methods, one of the best means of protection from car invasion is to have a CB system and know how to use it. Your call should be made directly to the police and not to anyone on the line. Channel 19 is the universal police channel.

On the Street

It's probably easier to get away from trouble when you are in a car than when you are walking. When walking alone you are vulnerable to attack from either another person on foot or from someone following you in a car.

Make it a habit to walk on the inside portion of the sidewalk, away from the street. Walk purposefully and with authority. An attacker is usually looking for someone who is timid and can be easily frightened or dominated. Looking assertive is a good preventative measure. An attacker may perceive you as a person who would fight violently if attacked.

Try not to look lost or confused— even if you are! Avoid walls, hedges, doorways, and buildings, and don't take shortcuts through alleys or darkened areas. If you have to, you can even walk in the middle of the street (when there's no traffic, of course) to get away from potentially dangerous side areas.

Sometimes your work or other activities will regularly put you in a dangerous street situation. For example, a woman who regularly works late at her office downtown may walk six blocks after dark to catch a bus or train to her home in the suburbs. If you are continually exposed to street danger, carry a small hand siren or some other kind of noisemaker. Keep your keys handy to use as weapons to gouge an attacker's face. Experiment with your keys to make certain that you can effectively use them like brass knuckles with one key placed between each finger.

Purse-snatching is more common than we like to think! So carry your purse with your arm through the handle or strap and hold it close to your body. If your purse has a long shoulder strap, wear it with the strap across your body.

If you are certain that you are being followed, cross back and forth across the street to make the person commit himself to a pattern. This technique demonstrates that you know you are being followed and are testing the follower; it just might discourage him. If your follower persists and you feel comfortable with the neighborhood, go to the nearest lighted house. Without going into the house, ask the occupants to call the police. Then wait on the lighted front porch until the officials arrive.

If the attacker does overpower you, remember not to yell, "Help!" People are more likely to come out of their houses if you yell, "Fire!" Outsiders also respond to breaking glass. If you have one hand free, throw anything within reach through the closest window—your purse, a shoe, a library book, a rock, or even gravel.

And of course, if you are attacked, kick, bite, scratch, claw, and pound while you are screaming. An assailant or robber does not want a wild woman on his hands!

Sometimes an exhibitionist or attacker will trick a woman into coming close to his car by claiming to need street directions.

Women have approached a car and discovered that the driver is wearing no pants. Or worse yet, she might come near the open window and find a gun pointed at her. Feel free to give someone directions, but keep a safe distance from the car.

The Neighborhood Dog

Although we're mainly concerned with human attackers in this book, we also need to be cautious of the nasty neighborhood dog. Almost every neighborhood has one, and the reports of attacks— mostly on children—are becoming much too frequent. Trusting children will approach a dog with joy. But many dogs are simply not trained to respond appropriately.

Dogs often feel threatened by strangers who approach them while they are protecting their home, owner, car, or puppies. They also shouldn't be bothered when they are eating, sick, or suddenly startled. In more bizarre cases, dogs have attacked family members without any provocation or obvious reason. In these cases, the animal is usually sick (possibly with rabies) or is becoming senile.

Some helpful hints
Never approach a car with a dog in it. Even a placid animal can become wild if you come close to or simply look at the car.

If you have to approach a house with a barking dog in the yard, pause and wait for the owner to come to the door to see what all the racket is about. Unfortunately, this can give the dog a feeling of "winning" because it is holding you at bay, and the dog could become more aggressive. You might try purposefully walking to the house, without seeming threatening to the animal. Use authoritative commands such as, "Stay!," "Sit!," and "Down!" Don't turn your back on the dog; face him all the way to the porch.

Remember, the most dangerous dog is a crouching one or one that is hiding in the bushes ready to spring.

The friendly dog

Some dog owners seem oblivious when their eager family pet, Wags, leaps on you, pawing and slobbering his affection. Dog lovers often don't mind, but if it bothers you, tell the dog's owner. Standing on the dog's hind foot is another way to limit Wags's loving leaps. If the owner isn't nearby to call off his pet and Wags persists in his overly enthusiastic behavior, bring your forearm up under the dog's jaw near its throat when it is descending from a leap. This should deter the animal more directly.

The stalking dog

Turn the tables on the stalking dog. If a dog seems to be stalking you, face it, bend down, and growl. Do this *before* the animal is close enough to bite you. In Rover's language, you're countering his threat with an attack of your own. Don't run or show fear; Rover loves a chase and can probably outrun you. If it looks as though Rover's attack is inevitable, grab the nearest object—a stick, a jacket, a rock—to throw at him as he closes in on you.

The attacking dog

When Spot attacks, he will leap upward, instinctively going for your face and throat. So use your legs and feet to reach Spot before Spot reaches any height. When the dog starts to leap, kick your foot into its face or ribs. Dogs are quick at avoiding strikes, so kick several times. Protecting yourself with your hands can be dangerous. Should Spot's jaws get close to your arm, ram your forearm forward into his throat as hard as possible. Keep kicking until Spot gives up and retreats.

When the dog bites

If Butch's teeth have grabbed your arm, hand, or leg, don't pull away from it! A dog's teeth slant backward, so a pull toward yourself will rip the skin. Instead, push inward toward Butch's throat. This will decrease the tearing action on your skin and will also gag the dog. If Butch gets close to your face, use both hands to grasp his throat as high as possible, with your thumbs gouging into his throat. Adrenalin should give you the strength to strangle the dog down to the ground. When your hands are high on his neck, Butch can't twist to bite you. If you continue with some blows and kicks, it won't be long until Butch wants to get away from you.

If you are bitten by a dog, write down the time and place of the attack. Catch the dog if possible, or write down which direction he went. Report the episode to the police immediately; if the dog is rabid, others might be in danger. Report directly to a physician or hospital for treatment and to arrange for aid in the event that the dog responds positively to a rabies test.

It's All in Your Head

You've determined in your mind that you can and will fight to protect the life and body God has given you. You have stored up all this background information about assaults and danger situations to become mentally prepared for any situation. It's all in your head! If you should be attacked (hopefully you'll never have to use all this information), keep your cool. That mental preparation is going to be one of your best escape advantages.

6

When It Happens to You

UNTIL NOW I HAVE TOUCHED JUST BRIEFLY ON WHAT TO DO IF attacked. My simple system is call on the name of Jesus out loud, then fight like fury! That's a very general treatment of self defense; of course, there are concrete, specific techniques to put to work in an attack situation. We've also established that there are as many types of attacks as there are attackers, so no two attacks will be the same. It takes a creative, cool mind to think while under attack, and the situation requires your concentration to help you escape.

A Weapon You Always Have with You

Your voice is one of the best weapons you have. If attacked, use it quickly and with a great deal of force.

The defense yell

It is possible to take force from your total body and explode all that energy into one loud yell. This is the "defense yell." Try it. Close your mouth and take a deep breath through your nostrils to fill your lungs. Then suddenly explode all the air through your open mouth while tightening your stomach muscles. Your whole body should tense as you yell, "NO!" in a loud, deep voice. You've probably heard people in the martial arts use the word, "Hiyah!" This yell is known as the "kei." When properly executed, the defense yell can have a frightening effect on anyone standing close by. The "kei" should accompany all blows and strikes to bolster the power of the hit. Because of adrenalin and concentrated body forces directed at one point, the smallest of women can execute a powerful and effective blow.

The defense yell which forces all the air out of the lungs has another benefit. If you are thrown to the ground or tripped, it will hurt more if there is air in your lungs. That air makes the lungs less flexible on impact. When you realize you are on your way down, a loud shout will help empty your lungs and make them flexible when you land. The choice is yours: either exhale that air yourself, or the ground will do it for you!

Of course, loud, general screaming can be effective because it attracts attention to you and your dangerous situation. So the defense yell is useful because it attracts attention, startles the attacker, and creates additional adrenalin flow to give you extra power. The loud, explosive yell should accompany each strike, blow, or movement.

A word of caution

As a general rule, yelling and screaming can be useful to thwart an attack. But there are a few times when you should be careful about using your voice forcefully.

If the attacker is holding a knife to your throat, don't yell! Yelling would cause too much body movement, and any neck movement could be painful or fatal.

If your assailant is pointing a gun at you, be quiet. I mentioned that one of the strong points of the defense yell is that it startles the attacker. In this case, you don't want to startle the attacker into inadvertently squeezing the trigger.

What you scream can also make a difference. Unfortunately, people won't always respond to a call for help. If you yell, "Fire! Fire!," people are more likely to come to your aid—even if it's just to make sure their own homes are not on fire.

Be a Detective

Your ability to recognize the characteristics of an attacker is critical to police work for the apprehension and identification of the criminal. Keep your mind clear. Be prepared to look for significant features and impressions.

Is your attacker male or female? What is his race? What about height, weight, and body build? Is he tall and thin, or short and stocky? How old do you think he is?

Hair is important! What color is the attacker's hair? What style does he wear it in? How long is it? Is it coarse and thick, or fine and limp?

How wide and how long is the attacker's nose? What color and shape are his eyes? Are they close together or far apart? Does he have a beard or a mustache?

Is your attacker's skin light or dark? What kind of complexion does he have? Does he have a scar, a tattoo, or any other distinguishing marks?

Voices vary a great deal. Does your attacker have any accent, lisp, or other speech impediment? Does he speak loudly or softly? Does he repeat phrases or use particular slang sayings?

What color and type of clothing does he wear? What style pants, shirt, jacket, and shoes is he wearing? Does he have a hat? Does he have any rings, bracelets, necklaces, or earrings? Is he wearing a hat?

Is he left-handed or right-handed? Does he have any noticeable gestures or mannerisms?

Does he have a weapon? Does he use it or threaten to use it?

Where exactly are you? Notice anything and everything about the street, the building, the walls, the floor. What time is it?

Which direction does he go when he leaves you? Does he have a car? What is the color, make, and model of that car? Can you read a license number? How many doors does it have? What color is the upholstery? Can you see any tears or stains in it?

Legal authorities recommend that, if attacked, you should try to leave your mark at the scene of the crime—on the attacker, on his car, in the place where you are attacked. If you're in a car, push a ring or some other item down into the space between the back of the seat and the bottom of the seat. A scratch on the attacker's face or arm will help in identifying the attacker through a skin match-up with the scrapings from under your fingernails. These small things can later help identify you as having been at the scene of the crime.

If you have been raped, your first impulse may be to run to the bathroom to clean yourself. Don't do it! It is absolutely critical that you do not change your clothes, bathe, or shower until you have undergone an examination. As deplorable as this delay may seem to you, the police need evidence to be effective in your case. An immediate interview should be conducted without changing the victim's personal circumstances.

Diversionary Tactics

No one can guarantee that any defense method will or will not work. But it is your responsibility to develop as many skills as possible. A specific skill might be successful in one situation, and totally fail in another. So practice various diversionary skills in the same way you practice physical skills. A skill that is practiced and often reviewed will come to mind quickly in an assault situation.

Talking

Talking (and getting your assailant preoccupied with conversation) is a powerful weapon. Let's talk about some things that work and a few that don't.

Remember, the typical motive of an assailant is to exercise violent power and domination, not to satisfy a sexual need. I've mentioned before that an attacker looks for a victim who will probably be easily intimidated and weak. So avoid begging, pleading, and bargaining. These tactics reveal fear and weakness and give the attacker the sense of power he set out to achieve.

Because of these same characteristics, it could be very dangerous to challenge the attacker's ego, masculinity, or honor. He obviously already feels threatened in these areas or he wouldn't be demonstrating his power and machismo through violent abuse.

Try to appear firm, positive, and in control. Don't take these characteristics too far, or your attacker may perceive you as derisive or brash.

Talk about his past and his family. If you hit on a subject that gets him talking, keep him on it! Conversation can distract him from his purpose of harming you.

You might make a comment about friends coming to pick you up, whether or not it's true. But whatever you do, don't make any threats of retaliation such as, "I'll go to the police. I can describe you. We'll get you. You'll go to jail for this." Believe me—your attacker doesn't want an eyewitness and the police hunting him down. Such threats could be fatal for you.

Most of all, remember the power of the name of Jesus. Talk to your assailant about the Lord, using the name of Christ as often as possible. Remember the incident of the missionary woman whose assailant ran away when she called on the Lord? Pray out loud! The power and peace of the Lord is available to you right in those moments of attack.

Actions

Be prepared to do any creative, bizarre thing that might open up an avenue of escape. Remember, the element of surprise is an excellent weapon in your defense.

Act like a lunatic— drool at the mouth, make faces, wave your arms, and quack like a duck.

Cough constantly, or vomit (on the assailant, if possible).

Go limp all over and drop in a faked faint.

Pretend you heard something—the telephone, footsteps, a whistle, or a siren. Or pretend there is someone else near or in the house by calling to an unseen husband, father, brother, or son.

I mentioned earlier that you might try to throw the nearest object through a window to create the sound of breaking glass.

Sometimes it even works to behave sexually aggressive, as if you want your attacker more than he wants you. This reverses his intended domination role. Outside the building where she took dance classes, a girl was accosted by a man who tried to force her into his car. The cool-headed girl melted her body against his and pretended to want to go with him. She told him she just needed to grab her purse, if he could wait for her for a moment. A minute later she was inside the building, locking the doors and shouting for someone to call the police. It may not always work, but if it's worked once it's worth an attempt.

Another woman awakened in the night to find a strange man standing beside her bed. He told her he was going to rape her. She quickly used her head. She acted aggressively, telling the man that she was willing but that she preferred her men to be clean. She pointed him toward the bathroom, and while he was showering she called the police. He was apprehended by the police (at least he was clean!).

If you're attacked, *think*! Then *do* whatever wild, distracting action that comes to mind. It could save your life!

The Four Stages of Defense

Wouldn't it be wonderful if there were one guaranteed method of escape for each and every attack? There is no such method, but there are measures a victim of attack can take to tip the scales in his or her direction in the event of an attack. The preventive actions and awareness of potentially harmful circumstances that we've worked through up to this point are at the forefront of great defense and attack avoidance. But if an attack is inevitable, I recommend these four stages for any person who is assaulted.

1. The first step is to *pray* —immediately and out loud. Go ahead and shout, "Jesus, help me!" Keep repeating that prayer. The name of Jesus has tremendous power to defeat evil. Call on his name.

This first step worked for Margo, one of my students. Believing that she had a chance to share the good news of Christ with an acquaintance, she went with him to his apartment. As soon as they were inside, he grabbed her and an assault seemed inevitable. She remembered the formula and cried out, "Jesus, help me!" three times. In their struggling, her assailant's shoe cut into her foot between the straps of her sandals. Suddenly she was furious and she screamed, "My foot! You've cut my foot!" The assault came to an abrupt halt as they both became distracted by her bleeding foot. He took her to the bathroom to clean it up. When she had doctored her foot, he told her to leave immediately—which, of course, she did. That is answered prayer—this time through a bleeding foot!

2. Do something *unusual*. Something that repulses your attacker is best. Become a wild woman, kicking and screaming. Become a crazy woman, rolling your eyes, lolling your tongue, and flapping your arms like a chicken. Cough, burp, sneeze, or vomit. Be creative!

3. *Fight*—with all your might and adrenalin. Strike, kick, scratch, claw, stomp, butt, scrape, and bite at any part of the attacker's body. Remember that you are not fighting to control or subdue, but you are fighting for space and time to escape. You need to inflict as much pain on your attacker as possible. Remember, it's a choice between your life and his injury. Decide right now how far you will go to protect the wonderful life God has given you.

4. Then *run*! If you manage to gain the space and time to escape, then run like the wind! Fear and adrenalin are still in your favor. You will run like you've never been able to before.

You may not be able to do all of these. You may not even be able to remember these four stages during the moment of attack. But at least remember to pray and to fight—in that order. God is with you—keep calling on him.

7

Pain Sends the Message

CONTRARY TO POPULAR BELIEF, SELF DEFENSE IN ITS RAW FORM is not necessarily any specific type of martial art. When self defense is mentioned, most people mentally picture Bruce Lee flying through the air dramatically posed in a kicking position. This visualization creates the false impression that self defense should be left to the highly skilled athlete. Actually, the opposite is true.

Self-defense skills can be effective for anybody anytime, whenever enough pain can be induced to stop an attack. True self defense is *anything* you can do to avoid an attack and *anything* you can do to get out of one. If a two-hundred-pound man reaches down to abuse a six-year-old child, the attack will stop immediately if the child pokes the attacker in the eyes. A little old lady with just a little knowledge is capable of kneeing a strong attacker in the groin and dropping him to the ground.

In an attack situation, there are no equal match-ups, no rules, no timeouts, no scores kept. It comes down to you and the attacker. You have to use every possible tactic to create pain anywhere you can on that attacker's body.

Pain

Pain becomes the factor which determines the success or failure of the attacker. In fact, it's so important to your self-defense knowledge and practice that we will deal with body pain points and how to deliver blows which cause pain in much greater detail later in this book.

An attacker uses pain or the fear of pain to subdue his victim. Early defense responses which inflict pain on the attacker help the defender avoid the attack and to escape a great deal of pain. Although most of us naturally don't want to inflict pain on another person, the defender has to create as much pain as possible for the attacker.

A universal language

Pain is a universal language —it sends a loud and clear message. It may seem vicious to you, but the medium of pain tells an attacker to stop the attack. How effectively you stop that attacker is directly related to your proficiency in physical defense skills. Practice will have brought accuracy and intelligence to your skills. The strength of your strikes and blows comes from those increased levels of adrenalin.

Of course you need to know how to "speak" this universal language, and this is what the rest of this book will tell you—how you can send the "Stop!" message with well-placed blows, kicks, and strikes.

Body Pain Points

There are numerous areas on the human body, male and female, which are particularly sensitive to blows and strikes. The top four are the eyes, the nose, the throat, and the groin. Areas where the skin stretches directly over bone are also extremely painful when struck by a blow because the bone cuts directly upward into the skin on impact. Some of those areas are the nose, the shins, the ankles, and the forearm. Let's make a quick overview of some parts of the anatomy that you may not immediately think of when looking for a place to strike.

The human head has some very tender places. Eyes, mouths, and ears are all possible pain points. The bridge of the nose (where the skin stretches over the bone), and directly under the nose are other spots. The temples and eyebrow areas are also skin-over-bone areas. The soft areas of skin under the chin and in the cheek area (where grandmothers and great-aunts pinch) are also potential pain points.

In one of my classes we had an unexpected demonstration of how tender and susceptible to pain the face is. In a rambunctious mood, a student named John decided to run, dive, and grab the leg of a female fellow student. When she saw him coming, she spontaneously drew her right leg back and then drove her knee upward into his face as he dived for her knees. The impact on John's face was so painful that he dropped to the floor, immobile and bleeding. Once I recovered from my surprise, I tended John's face. Then, as he lay recuperating on the floor, I gave a lesson on the powerful effectiveness of forceful blows to the face.

I mentioned that the throat was one of the top four body pain points. The chords in the throat, the base of the throat, and the epiglottis in the throat are all areas which are extremely painful when struck.

Blows to the solar plexus and the lower abdomen, in the stomach area, are a good deterrent for an attacker!

The groin area was also one of those four main areas. The genitals are extremely sensitive. The nerve endings at the inside of the upper thigh make up another tender place.

The groin area is not only sensitive for men. Did you ever ride your brother's bicycle or another boy's bike? If you were standing up while pedalling and your foot slipped from the pedal, you came down across the bar, straddling it. How that hurt!

Once a student checked with me to make sure she had mastered the knee lift to the groin. Of course I fully expected her to stop her blow short of the target, as she had been instructed. I went ahead and grabbed her in a bear hug from the front. She had the skill all right! To this day I remember the pain. Walking was painful for several days.

I'm sure that sometime in your life you've had a bruised, scraped, or broken leg or arm. You *know* how painful those "hurts" can be! The kneecap can be damaged by a direct breaking blow, a dislocating side blow, or a twisting of the joint. A kick to the shin or a scrape down the front of the leg can be terribly painful. The underarm is also a sensitive point. Elbow joints and wrists can be broken or dislocated.

Hands and feet offer more areas of distress! Broken or twisted fingers or a stomped toe could be all that's necessary to thwart an attack. The back of the hand and the top of the foot are two more skin-stretched-over-bone areas.

No doubt you are a nice person —the kind of person who doesn't normally spend a great deal of time considering how to inflict pain on another person's body. But it is important for you to consider the various pain points *before* an attack takes place —you won't have time to look them up when your life is in danger!

Auxiliary Weapons

If you are attacked, look around quickly to see what objects are available to use to defend yourself. Look for things such as furniture which you can place between yourself and the attacker.

Since you are that nice, normal person who has never focused on how to hurt another person, you probably don't see some everyday items as useful weapons. Think through some of these "weapons" to prepare a mental catalog which will be available to you in the event of an attack.

The noise of a siren, a whistle, or breaking glass can startle an attacker and possibly bring you some help.

Keys, combs, pens, pencils, a fingernail file, scissors, and screwdrivers are all sharp enough to hurt when jabbed at pain points.

You have probably never thought of a book as a weapon, but a direct, upwardly slanted blow to the nose can break the nose's delicate bones.

An umbrella, cane, broom, rake, shovel, fireplace poker, or a similar object can become a weapon for striking as well as for shielding yourself. A chair can also be a good shield.

You can strike with a flashlight, or simply startle an attacker with brilliant light in his eyes.

A coat, a towel, a purse, a belt with a buckle — all of these are potential weapons for self- defense.

Chemical solutions such as ammonia splashed or sprayed at an attacker might be one way to stop an attack.

Use your quick-thinking mind! Check out your home or apartment and consider the objects carefully—just in case.

The Best Weapons

These various tools and objects can be helpful, but the best weapons you've got are with you all the time. We've talked about some of these before.

Your *voice* is useful for screaming and for the defense yell. Like the siren or whistle, your shouts, screams, or whistles can startle an attacker and possibly draw some outside help for you.

Your *teeth* are good for biting and grinding. A bite to the fingers or back of the hand could loosen the grip that holds you.

Use your *head*—literally! Butt your head forward and backward into the attacker's face, his stomach, or another pain point.

Your *hands* can pull, hammer, and strike. Your *fingers* can scratch, claw, or twist tender skin.

Your *arms*, *elbows*, and *knees* can strike strong blows.

Your *feet* and *legs* can kick, trip, or scrape a shin.

No, you're not becoming the Bruce Lee image I mentioned earlier. But you're using your head. Self defense is using every part of your body and every ounce of your energy to protect yourself with "dirty street fighting." Remember that your best tools are with you all the time.

Levels of Response

God instructs us to be wise, and he has given us good minds with survival instincts in order to respond to threatening situations. Sometimes our very desire to demonstrate the fruits of the Spirit—peace, gentleness, etc.—makes us a perfect target for assault. For your own protection, you need to be aware of the evil which attempts to destroy a part of God's temple —your body. You are obligated, as his chosen vessel, to reject an attack against his Spirit.

Dealing early with any encounter is good defense. It is helpful in two ways: first, it might quickly intercept further involvement with an offender, and second, it puts you in some control of the situation.

The following suggestions may prove helpful in sending the message to an assailant that says, "Stop!"

Handling harassment

Hold your own when someone harasses you. If the offender is at a distance, ignore his comments. And mentally reject what he says to you, erasing it from your mind. It has nothing to do with you personally.

If the person is nearer and more difficult to avoid, respond with, "Get lost!" "No!" "Forget it!" "I'm not interested!" "I don't appreciate your comment." "Buzz off!" or "Beat it!" Repeat your response —the repetition and your firm stance might be effective.

Even if it seems silly to you, practice speaking statements such as these out loud when you are by yourself. They may not come naturally at first, but you'll want them to come naturally in the event of an attack. You might even have a close friend make ridiculous statements to you so you can respond with a loud rejection. You'll probably end up laughing, but the practice will help unlock some confidence and will increase your courage.

Restrainers

Now you're thinking, "But I'm a small woman!" or "I'm weak! I could never restrain a larger, stronger person!" It can be difficult, but restrainers can help you in those times when a child (a neighborhood bully or a child in a fit of temper!) or an attacking adult must be restrained to protect himself and you. These restrainers are moves which help you to control the movement of another person. We'll learn some of the basics later in this book.

Discouragers

Discouragers are moves which involve some injury (unlike restrainers). They might be useful in a date-attack situation, or an encounter with a neighbor or relative who mistakenly thought you might be interested in a physical relationship with him. Your response of a discourager— a shark bite (twisting the skin), a stomp on the foot, pressure on the nerves or joints, or a finger pull—might be all it takes to get rid of that unwanted interaction.

Injuries

Stopping a more advanced attack might require injury to the attacker. Striking, gouging, clawing, head butting, and breaking or dislocating the attacker's joints fall into this category.

Violent strikes and blows

Violent strikes and blows are called for when the motive of the attacker is life-threatening and his intentions are obviously brutal. Respond with the most violent blows you can muster. Your goal at this point should be to injure him in the most incapacitating way possible to allow an avenue of escape for yourself. This is no time for you to worry about your attacker's well-being— strike with force.

Principles of Strikes and Blows

Are you getting used to the idea of yourself as a fighter—a fighter who will protect herself and her family from attack? Here are some good fighting tips for you.

When you are accosted or grabbed, immediately concentrate on which appendage (arms, legs, feet, knees, elbows, head) is free to use for striking. If an attacker grabs you by your arms, your legs, feet, knees, and head are free.

When striking a blow, give it power by yelling a loud "no!" or "hi-yah!" You'll have to practice this technique a great deal, since the defense yell is not a natural reaction for you.

Avoid making wide, sweeping arm and leg movements while striking. They are easily detected and thwarted by an attacker.

As soon as your fist, knee, foot (or whatever) makes solid contact with an attacker's pain point, snap that striking hand or foot back instantly from the target. If you strike at sixty miles per hour, snap back at seventy! The receiver of your strike suffers more from a snap blow than when the striking implement (in this case, your fist or foot) stays in contact with the skin. This also puts that fist or foot into position to strike again.

Don't expect one blow to do the job. As you practice and your skills develop accuracy, practice successive strikes. Go slowly at first, getting faster as your precision increases.

Do everything you can to avoid being tied up. Being bound eliminates your fighting tools. Once tied up, you cannot fight against an attacker's brutality, and you may even be killed. Fight for your freedom.

Remember what you're doing—defeat is NOT your goal. Your immediate objective is to gain time and space.

Become proficient in kicking, kneeing, and stamping. Use of the legs, knees, and feet is one of the most effective modes of self defense. Your leg is much longer than an attacker's arm, so a kick with a fully-extended leg will reach the attacker before he can reach you. Your thigh muscles are the most powerful in the body, and an attacker will have difficulty stopping that kick. Remember to snap back when you kick. If you leave your leg or foot extended, an attacker might grab it or trip you to the ground.

Since knee and foot strikes come from the lower level of the attacker's vision, an attacker may have difficulty anticipating that strike. Use the knee or shin at close range, and the lower leg or foot at long range.

If you are held in a close bear hug from a frontal position, a knee lift to the groin can be effectively executed without having to see the target.

If you are kicking from the ground position, keep your knees bent and whip your foot up and into the attacker's face, groin, whatever, as he reaches for you. If you flail your feet and legs, he can grab them and control your movement.

While we're on the subject of kicks, consider five foot positions for kicking. Learn them now; they'll come in handy when you're trying out the kicks that are diagrammed in this book.

When you kick with a pointed toe, you kick with the top of the instep. The pointed toe kick is good for a kick to the groin.

If you want to kick with the ball of your foot, keep your foot flexed. You should use the ball of your foot to kick the solar plexus (stomach) and the lower abdomen.

If you're kicking with your heel, your ankle and foot should be flexed. A heel kick to the front, side, or area directly above the knee or to the shinbone can effectively incapacitate an attacker.

You can also kick with a flat foot or with the outer side of your foot. Flat foot kicks are useful for striking the chest, ribs, or knee or for a good, solid stamp on the foot. The side of your foot is useful for kicking on the shin.

Practice using the different parts of your body to deliver some strikes and blows. Hit a volleyball or a punching bag. These motions must be familiar to you so that they are immediately available when you are under attack.

Send That Message

Whether you send the "Stop!" message to your attacker by using a forceful comment, a restrainer, a discourager, an injury, or some forceful strikes and blows, send that message right away! Your immediate response takes some of the control of the situation back and puts the surprise factor back in your court.

Key to Diagrams

(A)	Attacker, Attacker's
(▲)	Front View
◯	Side View
(▲)	3/4 View
◯	Back View
(xx ᴧᴧ)	(A) in Pain
🦶	Pivot Foot

8

Basics of Balance and Control

*I*N PHYSICAL CONFRONTATION, ONE OF THE MOST SIGNIFICANT skills you may possess is your ability to maintain your balance. It is critical that you practice keeping your feet away from the attacker in order not to be tripped. You can train your feet to be quick enough to trip someone else — even a larger person. The key is learning pivot moves that provide a solid base for quick body moves and turns.

Basic Balance

Support and stability in stance
The broader the base of an object, the greater the stability. The object is more stable because the center of gravity is lower to the

ground. When the center of gravity of an object is tipped past the widest part of its base of support, the object will fall over (see Figure 8.1). Up to a point, the wider you stand, the greater your stability. You're bringing the center of gravity lower and spreading it out.

Figure 8.1 BASIC BALANCE: Support and Stability

a. The broader the base of an object, the greater the stability. The center of gravity (CG) is lower to the ground.

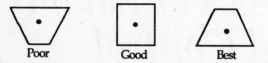

| Poor | Good | Best |

b. When the center of gravity of an object is tipped past the widest part of its base of support, the object will fall over.

| Supported | Supported | Tipped |

c. The wider a stance (to a point), the greater the stability.

 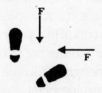

When a normal stance is taken and force is applied to a person's side, that person is tippable.

Force from the front will have the same effect.

A wider and slanted stance is favorable. It enables you to withstand force from many different directions.

If you stand the way you normally do, facing one direction with your feet parallel, you are "tippable" if a force is applied from the side or the front. But if you take a wider and slanted stance, you will have better support and will be able to withstand force from many directions (see Figure 8.1).

You can check to see if your weight is evenly distributed by first tapping your back foot on the floor and then tapping the front one. If you had to shift your weight considerably to do the tapping, you were out of balance.

Try this with a friend. Stand with your feet parallel, facing one direction. Have your friend push you from the front or from one side. Then widen your stance and put one foot back at an angle. Have your friend try to push you again. Which stance kept you in balance?

When you stand with one foot back at an angle and bring your center of gravity down lower, you are in a "fighting stance." This position turns the body sideways to the attacker, making it narrower. This protects vital parts of the body (chest, stomach, and groin) in the event of a direct blow. When you are in the fighting stance, that back foot is also in a position to drive forward with a hard kick or knee lift (see Figure 8.1).

Not that a natural stance is always the wrong one. Sometimes it's logical—for instance, if the situation is uncertain and potentially threatening and the attacker is facing you.

Do you play tennis or volleyball? Have you ever noticed what part of your foot you stand on when you're playing these sports? In most sports, you are taught to stay on your toes. The opposite is true in self defense. In self defense it is important to stay on your heels. Power is generated when the whole foot pushes off the floor or ground. Even when you're delivering a blow with your hand, the power comes from the heel of the back foot (see Figure 8.2).

Figure 8.2 BASIC BALANCE: Force and Ground Force

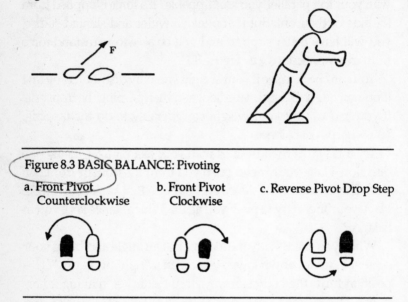

Figure 8.3 BASIC BALANCE: Pivoting

a. **Front Pivot**
Counterclockwise

b. **Front Pivot**
Clockwise

c. **Reverse Pivot Drop Step**

Pivoting your body is important in a fight—you want more than anything to stay out of the attacker's reach! You pivot your body by moving a foot and shifting your body (see Figure 8.3).

Practice pivoting with a partner. Stand facing a line on the floor. Make quarter and half turns, always finishing in the fighting stance. On the quarter turn, you should be at a right angle to the line. On the half turn, your back should be turned to the line. Have your friend slowly move toward you while you keep pivoting out of reach. As you get good at this, have your partner make faster lunges.

Staying on your feet

Your friend can help you practice staying on your feet, an important element in self defense. Find a soft surface, so you don't hurt each other when one of you manages to get the other down to the ground. Grasp each other's upper arms and hang on tight. Try to trip your friend, while trying not to be tripped (see Figure 8.4). Watch your feet! Keep them away from your friend. If at any point your leg is locked at the knee or ankle, step out of it immediately. Practice daily to keep "fast feet."

If someone grabs you, from the front or from behind, in a big bear hug, you tend to take a deep breath and hold it. That's a natural fear reaction. But in an attack situation, you want to make it as hard as possible for that attacker to hold onto you, so don't inhale and hold it. Instead, let all the air out of your lungs and go rag-doll limp, especially in the shoulders and knee joints. This makes you difficult to move (see Figure 8.5). Be limp first, then surprise him with your forceful attack.

Figure 8.4 BASIC BALANCE: Staying on Your Feet

Figure 8.5 BASIC BALANCE: Dead Weight

Tripping

It's great to understand how balance helps you withstand attack, but your knowledge of balance gives you another advantage: you know how to make an attacker lose *his* balance.

On a soft surface, practice tripping and being tripped with your partner. Go slowly and be accurate. You can be fast later; for now, make sure your partner is relaxed and non-resistive. When your partner loses his balance, hold on to him and lower his body slowly to the floor. Speed and force can be used in the event of an attack—you don't want to damage your friend!

If an attacker stands by your side with his arm around your shoulder, slip your closest arm behind him, and step with your closest leg across in front of him. Grab his far arm with your free arm and pull him forward, using your hip as a fulcrum. Keep your foot firmly planted and your leg solidly in place (see Figure 8.6).

If your attacker/partner bear hugs you from the front, step left, swing your right leg across and behind your attacker's legs. At the same time, bring your right arm up under his left arm, hooking

---

Figure 8.6 BASIC BALANCE: Tripping Forward

| Side by side. A arm on far shoulder. | Slip closest arm behind A. Step closest leg across front. Grasp arm. | Use hip as fulcrum. Pull the grasped arm. Push forward with arm behind. | Continue pull with foot firmly planted and leg solidly in place. |

across his chest. Grab his right arm with your left hand. Shove forward to push him backward, using your thigh as the fulcrum (see Figure 8.7).

If you are being pushed backward, grab your attacker's forearms and take a quick step backward while pivoting to the side. Fling your attacker on past you. It's not as hard as it sounds; your attacker's forward force should help you bring him past you (see Figure 8.8). Practice this with your partner.

Figure 8.7 BASIC BALANCE: Back Leg Crossover

Bear hugged from front; arms locked.

Step left, swivel hips. Hook right arm under A left arm across chest. Grasp A right arm with your left hand. Swing right leg behind A legs.

Your thigh is fulcrum. Push forward with your upper body to trip A back over the thigh.

Figure 8.8 BASIC BALANCE: Pushed Backward

Falling and rolling

When you're fighting, you end up in all kinds of unusual positions, and many of them leave you off balance. It is helpful to practice falling down and practice rolling out of unbalanced situations into a position of good balance.

Revert to kindergarten just for a few moments, and warm up by doing somersaults (forward rolls). If it's been a while, check out Figure 8.9 to remember how a forward roll is accomplished. As you come out of each forward roll, give the defense yell (the "kei"), slap out with your fist, and cock your knee. This is great practice for rolling out of an unbalanced situation and coming up ready to fight.

If you are falling sideways, curl your upper back in and your tail end under. Keep that chin on your chest. Lean in the direction of the fall, keeping your head forward. This gives you some control in the fall. Sit, and slap the ground surface hard with the hand and arm of the same side on which you are falling. That slap absorbs a great deal of the shock from the floor (see Figure 8.10).

If you are falling backward, make your body a "C" shape. The trick of falling backward without being hurt is the art of going

---

Figure 8.9 BASIC BALANCE: Forward Rolls

a. Kneel on the right knee with left foot flat on floor in front of your body.

b. Place back of right hand on floor, touching the ring and little fingers to the floor. Place left hand flat on the floor.

c. Tuck your head, chin on chest.

d. Push off with right toe and lift foot.

e. Roll along arm and shoulder.

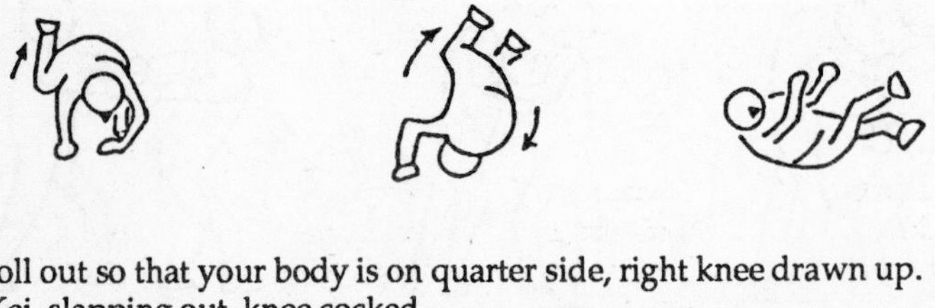

f. Roll out so that your body is on quarter side, right knee drawn up. Kei, slapping out, knee cocked.

with the motion. Keep that "C" shape. Don't reach back with the arms or hands—you may end up with broken or sprained fingers and wrists (see Figure 8.11).

Rolling can also help you throw your attacker. Now, you should not expect to throw a person over your shoulder. It *is* possible for a woman to throw a large person, but it is a risky move to practice without knowledge and supervision. If you enroll in a martial arts program, you will learn to complete a full throw.

If an attacker grabs you from behind while you are kneeling, grab his arms, tuck one of your shoulders in and roll toward that shoulder. Get one foot on the ground and leave the other knee on the ground, and roll sideways toward the kneeling side while holding the attacker's arms. You will have rolled him down with you in a position to get up quickly.

Figure 8.10 BASIC BALANCE: Falling Sideways

Figure 8.11 BASIC BALANCE: Falling Backward

| Curl upper back. | Tuck tail under body. Keep head forward, legs up. | Roll to shoulder. Keep chin on chest. | Slap hard on floor to absorb shock. |

If you are standing when the attacker grabs you from behind, drop to one knee with the foot of the same leg on the outside of the attacker's foot. Again, roll sideways toward that knee.

Basic Controls

Don't believe that you will be able to subdue a large man, or an angry man, or one under the influence of drugs and/or alchohol, by trying a submission hold on him. Submission holds only come into play after the attacker is already injured. These holds work well on a younger child who is out of control.

A submission hold is based on the principle of exerting pressure to cause extreme pain at one joint, usually forcing the joint into a direction that is unnatural and painful.

A good example is the simple thumblock. You force your attacker's thumb into the hand by exerting pressure on the first knuckle of the thumb.

Another is applying pressure to the neck chord. This submission technique is commonly called "The Spock" because the

---

Figure 8.12 BASIC CONTROLS: Wristlock #1

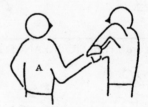

character of Spock from *Star Trek* used it to subdue his opponents with ease. If you pinch and lift the chords in the neck, it causes your attacker great pain. You can paralyze your attacker with this technique, or just drop him down to his knees.

The lip lock is simply grabbing the upper lip and pulling hard! That lip area is a tender spot, and your attacker will resist this painful procedure.

There are two wristlocks. In both, you are forcing the hand to bend at the wrist in a wrong (and therefore very painful) direction. If an attacker reaches for you, grab his hand with both of yours and place your thumbs on the back and middle of his hand. Bend his wrist so that his fingers point toward his shoulder (see Figure 8.12).

Use the second wristlock when your attacker is standing at your side. Manuever his elbow into your ribs, then place your hand over the back of his and press the joint. Your ribs stop that elbow from slipping past (see Figure 8.13).

Figure 8.13 BASIC CONTROLS: Wristlock #2

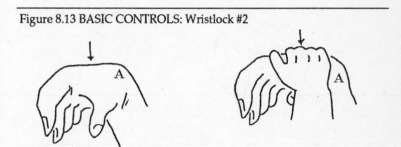

Figure 8.14 BASIC CONTROLS: Straight Arm Bar

Grab **A** wrist. Pull arm into a straight line.

Rotate **A** arm over with his elbow up.

Strike down just above elbow while pulling wrist up.

Another submission hold is the "straight arm bar" in which you "straighten" your attacker's arm, but not in the usual direction of the elbow. When the attacker reaches for you, grab his wrist and pull the arm into a straight line. Rotate his arm over so that the elbow points up. Then strike down just above the elbow while pulling up at the wrist (see Figure 8. 14).

In the head lock strangle, you wrap your arm under your attacker's head at his neck. Lean over the top of him, locking his head against your body. Reach your free arm under his armpit and grasp your forearm (outside to inside). Your arms now circle his neck tightly. Raise your arms slowly, choking your assailant (see Figure 8.15). When you practice this move with your partner, move very slowly, since this "strangle" can cause a blackout and ultimately death.

Figure 8.15 BASIC CONTROLS: Head Lock Strangle

Figure 8.16 BASIC CONTROLS: Arm Lock

Figure 8.17 BASIC CONTROLS: Arm Pin with Knee

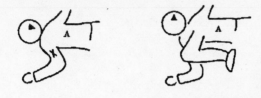

To "arm lock" your attacker, grab his wrist and place your opposite hand over, down, and under. Use your free hand to grasp your own wrist. You will have a tight hold of your attacker's arm in a position that is very uncomfortable for him (see Figure 8.16).

If you manage to get your attacker on the ground, you can pin his arm with your knee. Place the knee on a nerve spot just between his armpit and his elbow (see Figure 8.17).

These "basic controls" give you just that—*control.* You control by sending that pain message through these various submission holds.

Balance and control are foundational for the phsyical contact part of self defense. Practice keeping your balance and practice these control techniques with a friend. The fighting techniques we'll cover in the following chapters will build on this foundation.

9

How-to's for Hitting and Kicking

Y OU ARE ALREADY AWARE OF HOW IMPORTANT IT IS TO fight when you are attacked. This chapter should give you a wide range of ideas for ways to use your body to stop an assailant from harming you.

All of these strikes require practice. In practice you lose one element which would be in your favor during an actual attack: surprise. Of course your friend is expecting you to strike —that's what the practice session is all about. But your attacker intends to dominate you and is not expecting you to explode suddenly with kicks and hits. During practice, focus on accuracy; it doesn't do you any good if you practice incorrect movements. Remember to go slowly until you gain accuracy. And remember, pull up short of the actual blow; you don't want to lose a friend in the practice process!

Using Your Hands

I've encouraged you before to fight dirty if you are attacked. The situation is dangerous for you; you must do anything for an opportunity to escape.

Hands and fingers

The knuckle grind is useful in a couple of situations. If you and an attacker are in a handshake position, you can squeeze to inflict pain. If an attacker puts his hand on your body at any point, particularly on your thigh while you are seated, you can grind your knuckle into his hand. Make a fist, and thrust the knuckle of your middle finger upward. Curl your bent thumb outside your clenched fingers at the base of the upward middle knuckle for support. This puts your fist in a position to use that middle knuckle to grind (see Figure 9.1).

The shark bite is probably the easiest skill to accomplish, and it is very painful for your attacker. You can practice this on your own forearm. Form a claw with your hand, bending your thumb and

---

Figure 9.1 HAND & FINGER STRIKES: Knuckle Grind

fingers into a crab-like position. Tightly squeeze the skin between your fingertips and the heel of your hand and roll the hand forward, taking the skin with you (see Figure 9.2).

If an attacker places his hand on your body, grasp his little finger only and jerk it hard out and away from the other fingers to dislocate or break it. To give the yank further force, turn your body out and away from your attacker as you pull, still holding the attacker's little finger.

Another painful technique is to grab your attacker's neck, pushing your hooked thumb into the hollow of his throat while anchoring your fingers on the outside of the neck. Squeeze your thumb and forefingers together as hard as you can (see Figure 9.3).

A similar "hook" is the two-thumb eye gouge. When your attacker is threateningly close to your face, reach both hands up, anchor your fingers behind his ears, and hook your thumbs into his eyes (see Figure 9.4).

Figure 9.2 HAND & FINGER STRIKES: Shark Bite

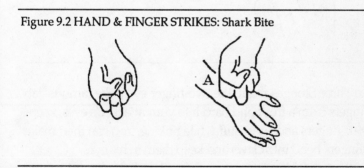

Figure 9.3 HAND & FINGER STRIKES: Thumb Hook in Neck

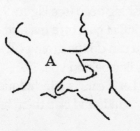

Figure 9.4 HAND & FINGER STRIKES: Two-Thumb Eye Gouge

Figure 9.5 HAND & FINGER STRIKES: Finger Hook at Neck Base

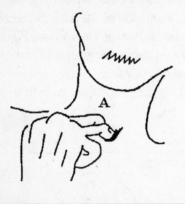

The Three Stooges made the two-finger eye poke famous. Jab two fingers from a free hand hard into your attacker's eyes, keeping your fingers and wrist stiff while poking. You can then make your fingers bend into claws and keep them in his eyes.

Another useful hook is accomplished by jabbing your first two fingers into the base of the attacker's throat, hooking them into the hollow of the neck and pushing deep (see Figure 9.5).

A very effective way to inflict pain on a male attacker is to grab in the groin and twist. You can do the groin pull and twist even when your attacker is standing behind you.

Clapping on your attacker's ears is a technique you may not have thought of. Cup your hands and clap them hard and fast on

Figure 9.6 HAND & FINGER STRIKES: Two-Hand Clap on Ears

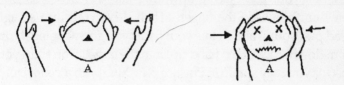

Figure 9.7 FIST STRIKES: Hammer to Nose

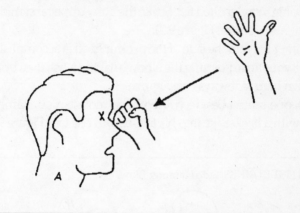

both ears. This procedure could possibly burst your attacker's eardrums or make him fall unconscious (see Figure 9.6).

Hair pulling is another good fighting technique. Grab head or facial hair and jerk hard away from the roots. If the hair is long, twist it as you pull.

Make a fist
Since most girls and women haven't spent a great deal of time punching things, many of them make a fist with their thumb curled up inside their fingers. That's a good way to damage your thumb! Learn to make a fist that can really send the message—to the nose, the solar plexus, or the ribs!

Draw your arm back with your wrist passing close to your waist and your palm facing upward. Make a clenched fist with your thumb outside the fingers. Then drive your arm straight ahead past your waist. Rotate your fist as you go, snapping the fist (palm down, back of the hand up) into the target. Don't curl your wrist, or you may sprain it. Practice punching with a volleyball or on a child's plastic, inflatable punching doll which bounces back up for the next hit.

Hammer on your attacker's nose, starting with an open hand and snapping to a clenched fist. Strike the bony upper and middle sections of his nose (see Figure 9.7).

A hammer blow to the side of the neck or head is accomplished by raising your arm, pointing the elbow, making a fist, then bringing it down hard sideways (see Figure 9.8).

If someone seated beside you bothers/molests you, hammer your fist with a backstrike into his face as you rise (see Figure 9.9).

Figure 9.8 FIST STRIKES: Side Hammer Blow

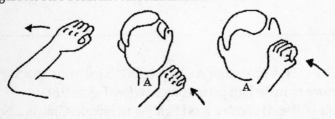

Figure 9.9 FIST STRIKES: Hammer Backstrike

You can numb your attacker's forearm or stop a blow by hammering his forearm. Bend your elbow with your hand open. Then snap down with a clenched fist, striking the bony part of the attacker's forearm (see Figure 9.10).

If you are grabbed around the shoulders from behind, step sideways and snap your clenched fist hard into the attacker's groin (see Figure 9.11).

Pug-hand hits
With fingers extended or very slightly curled, hold your hand so that it is at a right angle to your forearm. This pug position channels the power of the strike into the heel of your hand.

Figure 9.10 FIST STRIKES: Hammer to the Forearm

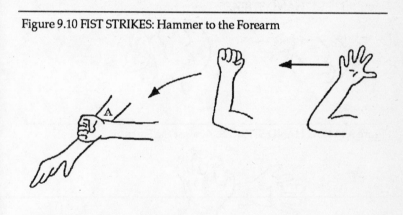

Figure 9.11 FIST STRIKES: Hammer to the Groin

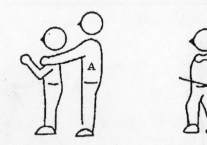

Use your hand in pug position by cocking your arm and driving the heel of your hand upward into an attacker's nose or chin with your arm fully extended (see Figure 9.12).

Numb the forearm or stop a blow by driving the pug hand into the attacker's forearm (see Figure 9.13).

Using Your Arms

Forearm blows
Your forearm's bony side makes an excellent weapon to use against the neck, forearm, or groin of your attacker.

Figure 9.12 PUG HAND STRIKES: To the Face

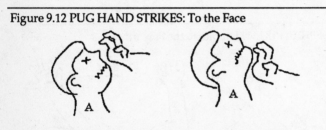

Figure 9.13 PUG HAND STRIKES: Against the Forearm

Figure 9.14 FOREARM STRIKES: To the Neck

Grab your own wrist and jamb the sharp edge of your forearm into your attacker's neck (see Figure 9.14).

Use the bony part of your forearm to strike your attacker's forearm just above the wrist. This blow will cause numbness and loosen his grasp (see Figure 9.15).

You can also cock your arm, clench your fist, and drive your forearm up between the attacker's legs to cause pain in the groin area (see Figure 9.16).

Elbow blows

The elbow is powerful and quick. Since it is used very close to the target, the attacker is usually unable to anticipate the blow to stop it. A well-placed, fast elbow to any part of the face is very effective and can disable a person quickly. The blow can be administered from any angle or plane as long as it is free to move.

Figure 9.15 FOREARM STRIKES: To the Forearm

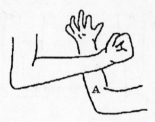

Figure 9.16 FOREARM STRIKES: To the Groin

The front uppercut elbow strike is accomplished by drawing your elbow back behind you, then swiftly driving it upward into the attacker's chin (see Figure 9.17).

If your attacker is standing behind you, draw your elbow forward and make a fist with your hand, then drive the elbow straight up and back toward the chin or the solar plexus (see Figures 9.18 and 9.19).

You can use your elbow to "sideswipe" your attacker in the head. If he comes at you from the front, draw your arm back and clench your fist, then snap the arm forward so that your elbow meets his head. If he comes at you from behind you, draw your arm forward, then snap it back (see Figure 9.20).

Figure 9.17 ELBOW STRIKES: Front Uppercut to Chin

Figure 9.18 ELBOW STRIKES: Back Uppercut to Chin

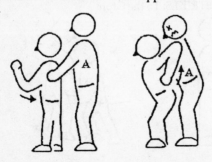

The rear side backswing is useful when an attacker grabs you from behind. Bend your arm and raise it with your fist clenched. Then drive your elbow sideways and backward into your assailant's face, chin, or throat (see Figure 9.21).

Using Your Head

Head butting is important when your arms are locked in a forward or backward bear hug or when your arms and legs are pinned. The head becomes a ramming weapon against the nose of the attacker. The force can be powerful enough to break your attacker's nose or shatter his cheekbone. Have you ever had a child sitting on your lap suddenly fling his head backward and catch you in the face? It hurts you much more than it hurt the child. Our heads are hard! Always remember to clench your teeth just before impact when you are using your head to strike. Otherwise you run the risk of biting your tongue or breaking your teeth.

Figure 9.19 ELBOW STRIKES: Back Uppercut to Solar Plexus

Figure 9.20 ELBOW STRIKES: Front Sideswipe

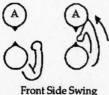
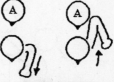

Front Side Swing
Top View

Back Side Swing
Top View

If your attacker grabs you from the front, cock your head back, clench your teeth, and snap your chin into your own chest, smashing your forehead into your attacker's nose (see Figure 9.22). You can practice this by having a friend hold a volleyball or nerf ball in his hands.

If your attacker grabs you from behind, cock your head forward with your chin on your chest, clench your teeth, and snap your head backward into his face (see Figure 9.23).

Using Your Legs

There are great advantages in using the leg and foot in kicking. The leg is longer and stronger than the arm, which makes it harder to stop a leg blow. Your legs are further below eye level, so your attacker has more trouble seeing the strike coming. A leg blow is more unexpected than an arm blow.

Figure 9.21 ELBOW STRIKES: Rear Side Backswing

Figure 9.22 HEAD STRIKES: Front Butt

We covered just briefly the types of kicks in chapter seven. They are kicks with the top of the foot (with a pointed toe), kicks with the ball of the foot (with your foot flexed), kicks with the heel of the foot (with the ankle and foot flexed), and kicks with the side of the foot.

Remember, after each snap kick, withdraw your foot as quickly as possible to avoid having your attacker grab your foot or leg and to prepare for the next kick.

Use the front snap, pointed toe kick to strike the attacker's groin. Draw your knee up as high as your navel, keeping the toes pointed downward. Snap the lower part of the leg upward and bring it back quickly. Plant your weight on one foot, and lean forward slightly over your stable leg while kicking (see Figure 9.24).

Use the front snap, flat foot to kick your attacker's groin, stomach, or knee. As he reaches for you, lean back and snap kick with a flat foot (see Figure 9.25).

Figure 9.23 HEAD STRIKES: Back Butt

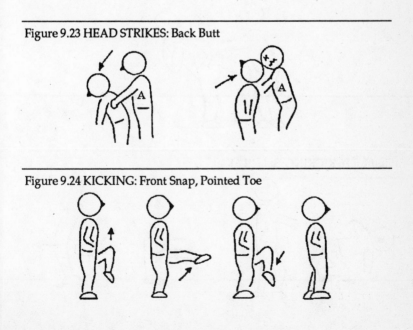

Figure 9.24 KICKING: Front Snap, Pointed Toe

If your attacker is reaching for you, you can lean over and deliver the side "T" kick. Lean and balance over the outside leg. Draw your knee up to your chest, then drive the flat foot forward into your attacker's closest knee (see Figure 9.26).

The backward donkey kick comes in handy when an attacker grabs your arms/wrists from behind. Draw your knee up to your chest, then snap forward at the waist while driving your foot back and up into the attacker's groin (see Figure 9.27).

When your assailant is standing close to you, you can use your foot to scrape down his shinbone with the outside portion of your shoe. Finish the scrape with a hard stomp across the top of the attacker's foot. This painful process can break the arch of his foot (see Figure 9.28).

When you are fighting and land on the ground, kicks are particularly useful. When your attacker reaches for you, your legs can

---

Figure 9.25 KICKING: Front Snap, Flat Foot

Figure 9.26 KICKING: Side "T" Kick

reach him before his arms reach you. Use one arm to protect your face. Keep your legs up off the ground, crossed just below the knees. When your attacker reaches toward you, snap the upper leg directly up into your attacker's forward knee (see Figure 9.29).

You could also lie on one side and hook your bottom leg behind the farthest leg of your attacker. Then explode with a direct kick

---

Figure 9.27 KICKING: Backward Donkey Kick

Wrist Grab   Draw   Drive Foot into Groin

Figure 9.28 KICKING: Shin Scrape and Stomp

Figure 9.29 KICKING: From the Ground, at the Knee

Figure 9.30 KICKING: From the Ground, at the Groin

Figure 9.31 KICKING: Knee to the Groin

with your upper leg into your attacker's groin. Not only will it hurt, it should knock him down (see Figure 9.30).

Your knees can also deliver some powerful blows at close range. If your arms are locked, place your hands on your attacker's thighs with your fingers pointed down and push. Drop your stronger leg back, then drive the knee up into your attacker's groin (see Figure 9.31).

If your attacker is coming in at you from the front, bent low in a fighting stance, raise your knee directly up into his face. At the same time, grab his hair or the back of his head to drive it down into your knee (see Figure 9.32).

Figure 9.32 KICKING: Knee to the Face

Keep practicing these fighting offensive moves until you have both speed and accuracy. The defensive moves require just as much attention and practice. We'll cover those in the next chapter.

10

Avoiding and Escaping

*T*HE LAST CHAPTER TAUGHT A GREAT DEAL ABOUT HOW TO use your body to strike and kick to inflict pain on your attacker's body. But we still need to discuss how you can avoid and escape painful blows and constraints.

Avoidance: Blocking Blows

Start by keeping as much space as possible between you and your attacker. When he begins to strike, step (or pivot) to the outside of the strike. Remember that at the end of a strike, your attacker's weight is thrown forward. That is the moment when he is most vulnerable to retaliation. Strike back at that moment with a quick, well-placed blow.

You need to be ready to block your assailant's blows. Stand in a non-threatening manner with one hand hidden. Grasp your own wrist, then let it fly up into a block position. You can practice holding and releasing your arm without your partner.

No matter what direction the blow is coming from, keep your arm between your attacker and your body. Make a fist. Strike up and out, making contact with your forearm against your attacker in an "X" fashion (see Figure 10.1).

You can also strike from the outside in, especially when blocking an upward thrusting blow. Pivot through as you strike, pushing your attacker's arm down with the force of your arm and your body. Immediately let fly your own strike (see Figure 10.2).

Figure 10.1 AVOIDANCE: Inside Snap Block

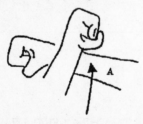

Figure 10.2 AVOIDANCE: Outside Snap Block

A strikes   **Block from outside in**   **Pivot through as you strike**

If your attacker is beating you around your head and face, place your hands on top of your head, and lock your elbows tight in front of your face. If you get a chance, when the time is right and your attacker is close enough, ram your knee into his groin (see Figure 10.3).

Practice snap blocking as a reflex to being accosted from behind. Have a friend tap you on the shoulder or back. Spin suddenly in a half-turn drop step to face your "attacker." At the same time, bring your arm up in a snap block (see Figure 10.4).

Escaping

Most attacks begin with a grab for the wrist and/or arm. You can learn to get out of the various grabs and holds that your attacker might put you in.

Figure 10.3 AVOIDANCE: Covering Your Face

Figure 10.4 AVOIDANCE: Practicing Blocks

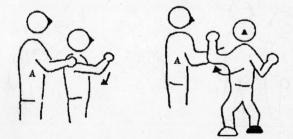

There are a few things to remember. First, an escape from a grab must always be accompanied by strikes, scratches, bites, and screams.

Second, keep thinking, "Which of my appendages is free to strike?" Before using a twisting move to escape a grab, strike hard. Then use your leverage and his surprise to help you escape.

And finally, remember that your power base for escaping a grab or a hold comes from a strong foot plant for leg power against the attacker's grasp.

Chest push

If your attacker comes at you from the front, grabbing your clothing in front or pushing you in the chest area, clasp both your hands over his hand on your chest and lock them tightly together. Bend forward suddenly. Your attacker's wrist has been bent in an unnatural and very painful position. He will usually drop to his knees (see Figure 10.5).

Wrist grabs

When an attacker grabs you at the wrist, your tendency is to put your arm straight to keep a wide distance between you and your attacker. Don't do it! Instead, bend your arm at the elbow in order to be stronger.

Figure 10.5 ESCAPES: The Chest Push

If only one wrist is grabbed, keep the other hand clenched in a fist and ready for striking. If both wrists are grabbed, use your feet for kicking and stomping.

Remember that the weakest part of your attacker's grasp is where his thumb and forefinger meet. That is the spot where you want to twist through to escape.

If your attacker grabs one of your wrists in one of his hands, twist the attacker's wrist toward your body and slip the slim part of your wrist through his thumb (see Figure 10.6).

Another option is to strike a hammer blow on your attacker's forearm just above his wrist. Then rotate your thumb counterclockwise toward your attacker's thumb up and over your attacker's arm. Make a fist and bend your elbow for more power (see Figure 10.7).

If your attacker uses both hands to grasp one of your wrists, step forward toward him. Make a fist of your captured hand, and

---

Figure 10.6 ESCAPES: Single Wrist, One Hand #1

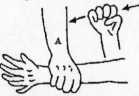

Figure 10.7 ESCAPES: Single Wrist, One Hand #2

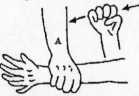

Hammer blow on **A** forearm.

Rotate thumb counterclockwise toward **A** thumb, up and over **A** arm.

Make a fist and bend at elbow for more power.

pull your elbow in toward your waist. Reach your free hand over the top of your attacker's arm, reach down and grab the fist of your captured hand. Push down with both arms and then jerk upward quickly. If unsuccessful, use that free hand to strike a blow (see Figure 10.8). Watch out for your friend's face when you practice this one!

If your attacker grabs your wrist when you are standing side by side, swing his arm up while rotating your hand up and out. Pivot a half turn toward him and swing your closest leg behind his

---

Figure 10.8 ESCAPES: Single Wrist, Two Hands

Make a fist of your grasped hand. Pull your own elbow into your waist.

With free hand, reach over the top of **A** arm, reach down and grasp the fist of your captured arm. Push down with both arms, then jerk upward quickly.

Figure 10.9 ESCAPES: Single Wrist Grab from the Side

Swing **A** arm upward.

Rotate your hand up and out.

Pivot 1/2 turn on your left foot and swing right leg in back for fulcrum.

Force arm back and down.

closest leg to act as a fulcrum. Then force his arm back and downward. You will have tripped your attacker backwards over your leg (see Figure 10.9).

If your attacker grabs both your wrists from the front, step toward him and bend your elbows for power. Rotate the thumbs of your clenched fists up and out, rolling over your attacker's grasp (see Figure 10.10).

If both your wrists are grabbed from behind, draw your knee up high, then snap forward at the waist and kick your flat foot into the attacker's groin (see Figure 10.11).

If your attacker has pinned you against the wall while holding your wrists, make both hands into fists and swing your arms downward sideways, the way you made "angel wings" in the snow as a child. Your arms sweep down along the wall. At the same time, bring your knee up swiftly in your attacker's groin (see Figure 10.12). This is another one you should be careful practicing with your partner!

Figure 10.10 ESCAPES: Double Wrist Grab from the Front

Figure 10.11 ESCAPES: Double Wrist Grab from the Rear

Figure 10.12 ESCAPES: Double Wrist Grab, Pinned to Wall

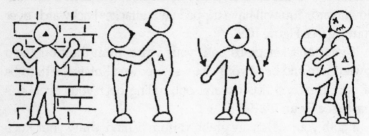

Figure 10.13 ESCAPES: Single Forearm Grab from the Front

Arm grabs
When an attacker grabs your arm, don't extend your arm and pull away. Just like when your wrist is grabbed, bend your arm to give it more strength.

When an attacker grabs your forearm from the front, bend your arm to pull yourself close to the attacker. Then come strong and hard with your other elbow and fist into his face (see Figure 10.13).

If he grabs your upper arm from the front, circle that arm out, up, and over your attacker's wrist, locking it against your upper arm. Quickly use your free hand to grab your own wrist and bend forward. You exert a great deal of painful pressure on your attacker's wrist (see Figure 10.14).

If one of your arms is grabbed from behind, turn around toward your attacker and grasp the captured hand with your free

Figure 10.14 ESCAPES: Upper Arm Grab from the Front

Circle grasped arm out, up, and over **A** wrist, locking it against your arm.

Grasp your own captured hand with your free hand and bend forward, putting pressure on **A** wrist.

Figure 10.15 ESCAPES: Single Arm Grab from Rear

Turn toward **A** grabbing your captured hand with your free hand.

Circle your grasped arm down, back, up, and over **A** arm.

hand. Use the strength of both arms to circle your grasped arm down, back, up, and over the attacker's arm (see Figure 10.15).

Your attacker might manage to twist one of your arms into a hammerlock hold behind your back. If this happens, you can reach back with the free hand and push down hard on the captured wrist. Otherwise, step forward with the foot opposite the arm that is being held, bending at the waist to extend your arm. Pivot toward your attacker on the back foot and strike! Use your free fist or elbow to land a solid blow (see Figure 10.16).

Figure 10.16 ESCAPES: The Hamerlock Hold

Back View   Side View   Reach back   Step forward with
                              with free   foot opposite the cap-
                              hand to push   tured arm. Bend at the
                              down on cap-   waist to straighten
                              tured wrist.   your arm. Pivot to-
                                               ward **A** on back foot,
                                               and strike.

Figure 10.17 ESCAPES: Armlock from the Side

If your attacker puts you in an armlock, grabbing your arm and
locking it at the elbow, release the painful grip by pushing the
attacker's elbow forward and pulling your captured arm backward. At the same time, kick and keep kicking the side of the
attacker's knee (see Figure 10.17).

When your elbow is grabbed from the front, swing your arm
up, out, and then back over your attacker's forearm. Jam your fist
and arm down hard across his forearm, twisting out of the thumb
grip (see Figure 10.18). If both elbows are grasped, clench your
fists and make the same movement with both arms at once. Bring
your arms around and down hard on your attacker's forearms
while twisting out of his grip.

Figure 10.18 ESCAPES: Elbow Grab from the Front

Make a fist. Swing your arm up, out, and then back over **A** forearm.

Jam your fist and arm down hard across **A** forearm, twisting out of the thumb grip.

Make fists. Swing your arms up, out, and then back over **A** forearm.

Jam both fists and forearms down hard across **A** forearms.

Figure 10.19 ESCAPES: Elbow Grab from the Side

If he grabs your elbow from the side, make a fist and rotate your arm up and backward over the forearm of the attacker. Keep rotating until his grip is released (see Figure 10.19).

Should an attacker grab one of your elbows from behind, step backwards on the same side as your captured arm. Pivot on that

Figure 10.20 ESCAPES: Single Elbow Grab from Rear

| Step back and pivot on the side of the captured arm. | Cock your free arm while turning. | Drive off back foot with pug hand into A face. |

Figure 10.21 ESCAPES: Double Elbow Grab from Rear

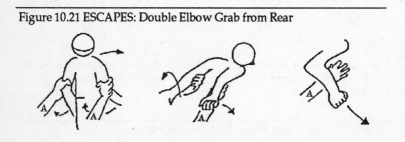

foot, cocking your free arm as you turn. Drive off the back foot with a hard pug-hand blow into the attacker's face (see Figure 10.20).

If both your elbows are being grasped, lean forward and raise your arms on the inside of your attacker's arms. Swing your fists and arms over the top of his and thrust out and down (see Figure 10.21).

Shoulder grabs

If an attacker grabs one of your shoulders from the front, give his grasping hand and wrist some pain. Reach across with your free hand and grab his little finger. Pull the little finger clockwise over

Figure 10.22 ESCAPES: Shoulder Grab from Front

Reach across with your free hand to grasp A little finger and pull counterclockwise.

Rotate A little finger over the thumb until palm faces up, wrist bent.

Press on back of A hand with both thumbs.

Figure 10.23 ESCAPES: Double Shoulder Grab from the Front

Throw both arms up on the inside of A arms. Go out around and down past A arms.

Hook A arms and come up on inside, circling up, out, and around, and hook under A arm.

the thumb until his palm is facing up. This bends the wrist into a painful position. Dig in with your thumbs into the back of your attacker's hand (see Figure 10.22).

If both your shoulders are grabbed from the front, throw both your arms up between the attacker's. Go on out and around and down past his arms. Hook his arms and come up on the inside, making a circle with your own arms. Follow the circle around, coming up on the inside, out, and around, and hooking under the attacker's arm. Your attacker will not be happy to find his arms twisted! (See Figure 10.23).

When someone grabs your near shoulder from the side, circle your arm vigorously up and back, down and under your attacker's arm. Hook his arm at the elbow and lean backwards (see Figure 10.24).

If your far shoulder is grabbed from the side, with your attacker's arm around you, jab your near elbow hard into his solar plexus. Step your near foot behind his legs to act as a fulcrum against his thighs. Fling your close arm up and across your attack-

---

Figure 10.24 ESCAPES: Near Shoulder Grab from the Side

Make a vigorous arm circle by swinging captured arm up and back and down and under **A** arm.

Hook **A** arm at the elbow and lean back.

Figure 10.25 ESCAPES: Far Shoulder Grab from the Side

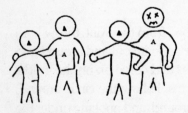 

Strike your elbow into **A** solar plexus.

Step near foot behind **A** legs. Fling your closest arm up and across **A** just below the neck.

er right at the neck. You'll push him backward over your leg and land him on the ground (see Figure 10.25).

If both your shoulders are grasped from the rear, reach down backward between your legs to grab one of your attacker's ankles with both hands. Rise up quickly, jerking his ankle up. Stand up straight then lean back, causing the attacker to fall backward (see Figure 10.26).

Another way to handle being grabbed by both shoulders from the rear is to step to the side, placing your closest thigh or side behind the attacker. Your body should be in contact with the attacker's backside. Reach down across both legs and place your hands behind his knees, putting your shoulder into the attacker's chest. Jerk the knees up, throwing that shoulder back into the at-

---

Figure 10.26 ESCAPES: Double Shoulder Grab from the Rear #1

Figure 10.27 ESCAPES: Double Shoulder Grab from Rear #2

Rear grasp. Step to side. Place closest thigh behind **A** backside. Reach across and place hands under **A** knees. Raise the knees and push your shoulder back into **A** chest.

tacker. This should fling him backwards over your leg (see Figure 10.27).

Head grabs

If your mouth is being covered by one or both of your assailant's hands, reach up and grab his little fingers, putting your thumbs underneath and your fingers on top. Jerk up and away. You'll probably break his fingers (see Figure 10.28).

If an attacker pulls your hair from the front, reach up and clasp your hands over your attacker's to keep pressure off his pull. Clasp your hands on the attacker's wrist (or wrists) on your head, then snap your head forward. This forces the hand back in a position that causes pain to the attacker's wrist (see Figure 10.29).

If he pulls your hair from the back, clasp your hands over his. Step backward toward the assailant with your head down. Pivot a half drop step to face your attacker. Then bring your head up

---

Figure 10.28 ESCAPES: Hand Over the Mouth

Figure 10.29 ESCAPES: Hair Pulled from the Front

suddenly to release his grip. If you are sitting down when your hair is grabbed from the back, clasp your hands on his. Stand and turn, twisting under your arm so that you are facing the attacker (see Figure 10.30).

If you have long hair, an attacker might grab and pull from behind. If this happens, clasp your hands on your head to relieve the pressure on your hair roots. Do a half turn toward your attacker, bending down while turning and keeping your hands on your head. Rise up suddenly and strike (see Figure 10.31).

Figure 10.30 ESCAPES: Hair Pulled from the Rear

Clasp your hands over **A** hand. Step back toward **A**, head down. Pivot a half-drop step to face **A**. Suddenly raise your head.
If seated:

Grasp **A** hand with both of yours. Stand and turn, twisting under your arm to face **A**. Suddenly raise your head.

Figure 10.31 ESCAPES: Long Hair Pulled from Rear

If your attacker is holding you from the side with your head locked under his arm, turn your head toward him to release the pressure, stomp on his foot, and smash your fist into his groin.

Chokes

When you are grabbed around the neck, immediately tense up the muscles in your neck, drop your head down, and turn your head sideways to take the pressure off the windpipe. Since choking and tripping often go together, step backward in an attempt to keep your feet away from your attacker.

Figure 10.32 ESCAPES: Single-Hand Choke from the Front

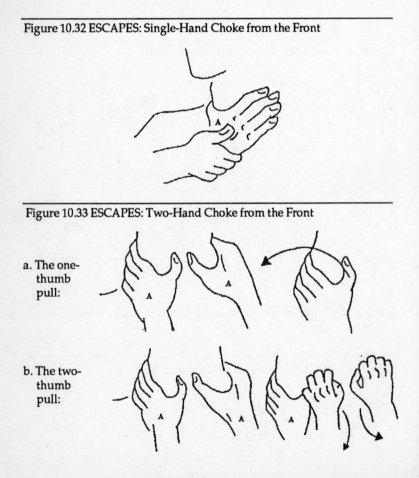

Figure 10.33 ESCAPES: Two-Hand Choke from the Front

a. The one-
   thumb
   pull:

b. The two-
   thumb
   pull:

If he grabs you with one hand from the front, reach across his arm and dig your thumb in the middle of the back of your attacker's hand, holding on to the hand with your other fingers. Jerk the hand violently so that the little finger rotates up and over toward his thumb (see Figure 10.32).

If he grabs your neck with both hands from the front, reach over his hands and grab one of his thumbs. Yank it quickly in an outward and downward motion. Pivot your body toward the pull, dropping on your knee that is closest to your attacker. Keep rotating his thumb and hand over his wrist (see Figure 10.33). You could also try reaching up between his hands, grabbing both thumbs, and jerking them downward.

Figure 10.34 ESCAPE: Two-Hand choke from the Front (Figure Eight)

Place your right arm over **A** left arm. Bring your left arm under **A** right arm. Grasp your hands together in a figure eight.

With a snap movement, force your upper arm down and lower arm up. Turn toward the downward movement to break the hold.

Figure 10.35 ESCAPES: Two-Hand Choke from the Front (Windmill)

Another way of escaping the two-handed choke from the front is to bring your right arm up and over your attacker's left arm, and your left arm in and under his right. Clasp your hands together. Snap your upper (right) arm down and the lower (left) arm down, turning toward the downward movement to break the hold (see Figure 10.34).

You might also try what I call a "Windmill." Step forward toward your choking attacker. Make a fist, and fling your arm in a high circular motion over his arm. At the same time, swing your forward foot in a half circle, pivoting on the back foot. Keep pivoting, then bring your shoulders and hips through your attacker's arms (see Figure 10.35). Follow through with an elbow strike.

If your attacker chokes you from the front with his arms bent, his face comes very close to yours. Reach between his arms and

Figure 10.36 ESCAPE: Two-Hand, Bent-Arm Choke from the Front

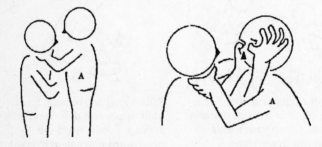

Figure 10.37 ESCAPES: Two-Hand Choke from the Rear (Little Finger Pull)

clasp your hands on the side of his head. Gouge your thumbs into his eyes (see Figure 10.36).

If you are being choked from the rear, reach up in front and grasp the attacker's little fingers. Jerk away from the pressure on your neck (see Figure 10.37).

You might try a "Reverse Windmill" when being choked from behind. Raise your arm up straight, making a fist. Drop step toward your assailant, pivoting your body through his arms. Follow through the pivot, circling your arm down and over to lock your attacker's arms down against your side. Use your free fist or elbow to strike a blow to his face (see Figure 10.38).

Another technique for escaping the two-handed choke from the rear is the "Reverse Bow." Drop step one foot behind the other in a full half turn counterclockwise. Plant your feet firmly and bow toward your attacker while turning. Rise up suddenly, ready to strike (see Figure 10.39).

Figure 10.38 ESCAPES: Two-Hand Choke from the Rear (Reverse Windmill)

Figure 10.39 ESCAPES: Two-Hand Choke from the Rear (Reverse Bow)

Figure 10.40 ESCAPES: Two-Hand Choke from the Rear (Arm Wring)

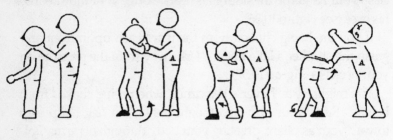

Figure 10.41 ESCAPES: Two-Hand Choke from the Rear While Seated

Try the "Arm Wring" to escape a two-handed choke from behind. Grasp one of your attacker's wrists with both of your hands. Hanging on tight, do a drop step with the opposite foot, turning to face him. Wring his arm in one direction like a rag (see Figure 10.40).

If you are seated when an attacker chokes you from behind with both hands, reach across with one hand to grab your assailant's opposite wrist. Use your free hand to grab his same arm at the elbow. Pull his wrist toward you and push the elbow up. Rise from your seat and pivot away from his elbow, pulling your head out. Finish this move with an arm wring (see Figure 10.41).

If your attacker is choking you from behind with his forearm, quickly turn your head toward his elbow, taking the pressure of his forearm off your windpipe. Yank his arm down with both hands, and strike with kicks and blows to his groin, stomach,

Figure 10.42 ESCAPES: Forearm Choke from the Rear #1

Bend over. Swivel hips to the
side. Step closer leg behind **A**.

Squeeze your head back through
A arm. Rise up and fling your
arm across **A**.

Figure 10.43 ESCAPES: Forearm Choke from the Rear #2

knees, feet, and head. Try to push his arm off with the heel of your
hand at his elbow.

You might try turning your head toward his wrist, bending
over and swiveling your hips to the side. Step your closer leg behind your assailant's. Then squeeze your head backwards
through and under his arm. Stand up straight and fling your close
arm hard across his chest, pushing him backwards (see Figure
10.42).

Another technique is to turn your windpipe toward your
attacker's elbow, while reaching back with one hand to jerk his
hair backward. Strike hard with the other hand at the same time
(see Figure 10.43).

Figure 10.44 ESCAPES: Chokes with a Rope or Other Article

Your attacker might use a rope, a cloth, wire, or nylons to try to choke you. If this happens, hook your fingers onto the choking material immediately to release some of the pressure. Turn your head toward your attacker, pivoting with a backward drop step. Raise the arm closest to him to take off pressure. Once you are facing him, release one or both hands from the rope or cloth to strike. You will probably receive rope burns from this (see Figure 10.44).

Reaches
When an attacker reaches for you and you see him coming, you can do one of two things to protect yourself from being grabbed in the first place. The first is to clasp your hands together and bring your own arms up between your attacker's outstretched arms, knocking them away. You might also try leaning away to keep your upper body from his reaching arms, shifting your weight onto your back foot and cocking the forward knee close to your chest. Drive the bottom side of your foot straight into your attacker's knee to hyperextend it (see Figure 10.45).

Bear hugs
There are four types of bear hugs. You could be "hugged" from in front with your arms free or hugged from in front with your arms pinned. You could also be bear-hugged from behind with your

Figure 10.45 ESCAPES: Reaches

a. Wedge Block:

b. "T" Kick:

arms free or pinned. In any bear hug hold, take a deep breath and bend your knees to make your body dead weight, and kick.

If you are being held from the front, but your arms are "unlocked," you can shove your forearm or dig your fingers and thumbs into your attacker's throat, knee his groin, pug hand or hammer blow his nose, use the two-finger poke in his eyes, use your elbows to strike his face, kick his knees or his groin, or try the crossover trip.

If your attacker does have your arms pinned, you have fewer options. Grab the skin at his waist with your hands and shark bite. Or place the palms of your hands on the front of the attacker's thighs with your fingers pointed down. Stiffen your arms and push against his thighs, while extending your right leg back. Drive that right knee up and forward into your assailant's groin.

Figure 10.46 ESCAPES: Rear Bear Hug, Arms Unlocked

Figure 10.47 ESCAPES: Rear Bear Hug, Arms Locked #1

When someone grabs you from behind but leaves your arms free, use your elbows to smash into his face. Scrape his shin with your shoe, and stomp on his foot. You might also try stepping forward with one foot while using the opposite elbow in a blow to the face. Turn your upper body with the elbow up toward the attacker while striking. Turn quickly and repeat with your other elbow on the other side of his head (see Figure 10.46).

If you are being bear-hugged from behind with your arms pinned at your sides, butt your head backward into your attacker's face. Scrape his shin with your shoe, and stomp on his foot. Reach in behind you, and twist and pull in the groin area. You might try lowering your body while raising your arms to create space. Step to the side, and drive your elbow into your attacker's stomach or hammer into his groin. If you can, step behind him and trip him (see Figure 10.47).

Figure 10.48 ESCAPES: Rear Bear Hug, Arms Locked #2

Figure 10.49 ESCAPES: Full Nelson Bear Hug

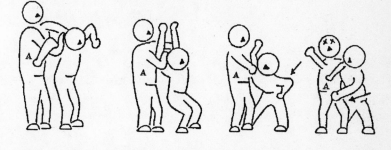

You could also try to swivel your hips and step behind your attacker with your closest leg, placing your foot flat between his feet with your thigh to his backside. Snap forward at the waist, pulling the attacker with you. Then suddenly straighten, flinging your arm up and backward right under his chin to throw him backward (see Figure 10.48).

Another way to escape a rear bear hug when your arms are locked is to reach down between your legs and jerk up on your attacker's ankles. This is the same technique used for a two-handed shoulder grab from behind (see Figure 10.26).

If you are bear-hugged from behind with your arms pinned and your body is picked up off the ground, try to swivel your hips and strike your fist backward into your attacker's groin.

A full-nelson is a wrestling hold in which your attacker has his arms under your arms at his elbows with his hands behind your head, pushing your head forward. If you are being held this way, shoot your arms straight up and sink down, pulling your arms out of the hold. Drop step with one foot, twisting toward your attacker, then smash your fist into his groin (see Figure 10.49).

Practice blocking blows and escaping grabs and holds with a friend, slowly at first and with increasing speed as you gain accuracy. Be careful not to hurt your friend with the blows and kicks which immediately follow these block and escape moves.

11

Some Special Circumstances

YOU PROBABLY KNOW MORE ABOUT FIGHTING NOW THAN YOU ever expected to! You've been practicing balance and control, hitting and kicking, and avoiding and escaping. I'd like to mention a few more circumstances that could come up so that you will have covered in your mind and in practice as many potential attack situations as possible before any attack ever happens.

When You're Sitting Down

We all spend a lot of our lives sitting down! Attacks can happen while you are seated. Think, for example, of sitting at a bus stop or on a public transportation vehicle. You don't know that person sitting next to you. You could be attacked by someone you never expected to trouble you—we've already discussed date/acquaintance rape.

We've talked a bit about what to do if your hair is pulled or your shoulders are grabbed while you are sitting down. Remember that if someone puts his hand on your leg, you can reach down and yank his little finger back, possibly breaking or spraining it. You could also dig into the back of his hand with a knuckle grind or deliver a hammer blow to his nose.

Another good response to a hand on your leg is a quick elbow blow to his face or ribs. You might just strike backward on his forearm to sweep his arm away from you. You could grab the muscles and nerves in your attacker's upper inner leg. Remember you can finger-poke his eyes or windpipe or send a pug hand up into his face.

If someone sitting next to you puts his arm across your shoulders with his hand on one shoulder, reach across your own body with the arm that is closest to him and grab his little finger. Lift your attacker's whole hand up, stand up, and go under his arm counterclockwise. You will twist his arm and hand and cause him great pain (see Figure 11.1).

Lunges

An attacker might lunge at you to grab you or to knock you down. If an attacker dives for your lower body, cock your back leg and

---

Figure 11.1 SEATED ATTACKS: Arm Across Shoulders

then drive that back knee forward into his oncoming face. The force of your leg coming forward meeting the force of his face coming forward will produce quite an impact (see Figure 11.2).

If you are grabbed around the knees, grab your assailant under his neck and armpit, lock your arms and roll backwards, flipping him.

If your attacker lunges at your ankles, kick hard into his face. You could also slip backward and violently push his head and upper shoulders down into the ground with both your hands. Follow this up with blows and kicks (see Figure 11.3).

On the Ground

Sometimes it's just impossible to stay on your feet. An attacker's force and power might land you down on the ground. Review the section on balance and control to remember how to fall so that you are ready to get up quickly or to strike from a ground position.

Figure 11.2 LUNGES: At Your Thighs

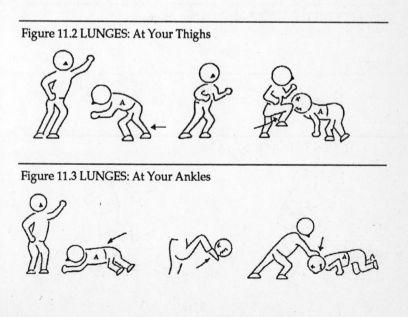

Figure 11.3 LUNGES: At Your Ankles

Distant Approach

If you can see your attacker coming toward you, you can deliver an attack of your own on his knee. For example, if he steps toward you with his right foot, roll to your left hip and hook his forward foot at the inside ankle with your left foot. Then drive your right (upper) foot forward with force into your attacker's knee. Push with your right foot on that knee while you pull on his hooked ankle with your left foot (see Figure 11.4).

Near Approach

If your attacker is approaching you from very close to you, grab the ankle closest to your body with your hand, and jam the opposite foot into his knee, pushing hard (see Figure 11.5).

Your attacker may kick you while you are on the ground. Bunch yourself up into a ball to protect your face and stomach. This position makes you hard to pick up and unfold. This position also puts your legs into a cocked position, ready for delivering forceful kicks whenever that attacker leans over you.

Figure 11.4 ON THE GROUND: A Distant Approach

Figure 11.5 ON THE GROUND: A Near Approach

If your attacker is pulling or dragging you by one foot, use the heel of the other foot to keep jamming down on the thumb and fingers holding your foot. When you are being dragged by one or both ankles, pull your body closer to your attacker and pull his ankles toward you while pushing away with the leg he is dragging. This should throw him off balance.

If you are being choked while pinned on the ground with your attacker kneeling at your side, raise the arm farthest from him and reach across both of his wrists to grab the opposite wrist. Bend your opposite leg and plant your foot firmly. Pull back toward your attacker while rolling your hips over violently to break away from him (see Figure 11.6).

If your attacker has pinned and straddled you and is choking you, try to use your head to butt his nose and your hands to gouge his eyes or strike his face. Bring your flat feet up under your hips, thrusting your hips upward. This should force your attacker forward and upward. Turn your face to the side, and then swing your arms up and roll your hips swiftly to one side. Follow this with a forceful strike, then run (see Figure 11.7)!

If you are on the ground with your attacker beside you pinning you at the wrists, raise the knee of the leg farthest from your at-

---

Figure 11.6 ON THE GROUND: Pinned and Choked from the Side

Figure 11.7 ON THE GROUND: Pinned, Straddled, and Choked

tacker with the foot flat on the ground. Push off from the ground and roll over, throwing your outside knee up into his groin (see Figure 11.8).

If you are pinned at your arms to the ground and straddled at the hips by your attacker, snap your arms down to your sides (in "angel wings" fashion) while thrusting your hips upward. Your feet should be in tight and close to your hips, and your back should be arched. Roll your head to the side, then do a side shoulder roll (see Figure 11.9).

If you are lying face down and your attacker approaches to roll you over, swing your farthest leg out and away, forming a wide angle with your legs. Push off with your outer leg and swing your head and shoulders toward your attacker's legs, reaching in and grabbing for his knee or ankle. Lock your arms behind his leg or ankle and pull yourself up ready to strike.

Stay off the ground as much as possible. Get up as quickly as possible —to your knees if you can't manage to rise to your feet. Always keep your hands up to protect your face.

Figure 11.8 ON THE GROUND: Pinned at the Wrists from the Side

Figure 11.9 ON THE GROUND: Pinned, Straddled at the Hips

Weapon Attacks

Attackers will often use a weapon to threaten you or to hurt you in order to make you submit to their violence.

There are a few general principles to remember when fighting a knife or another instrument used to stab or strike. First, watch your attacker's grip. His grip on the weapon determines the angle of the thrust. If he is gripping the knife with the blade down, his thrust will be downward. If he is gripping the knife with the blade up, the thrust will be upward. Second, turn your body sideways to protect vital organs. Third, of course, stay as far away from your attacker as possible, placing objects or furniture between you. Fourth, wrap a piece of clothing or any other cloth article around your arm to protect you from being cut when you strike your attacker. And finally, remember that your attacker is most vulnerable to attack at the end of his knife thrust. Move outside his knife when he thrusts, and then strike.

If your attacker strikes from the front, do a sidestep and a very quick "T" kick to his knee before he can draw back (see Figure 11.10).

If he comes at you with an overhead stab, you have a couple of options. If you can, keep your distance and cover your arms. As your attacker stabs downward, step back with your right leg, flat foot. At the same time, cross your arms at the wrist. Absorb the blow in the cross of your wrists, and follow it with a quick, force-

---

Figure 11.10 WEAPON ATTACKS: Knife, Front Thrust

Figure 11.11 WEAPON ATTACKS: Knife, Overhead Stab #1

Figure 11.12 WEAPON ATTACKS: Knife, Overhead Stab #2

Forearm block.

Run your other hand under **A** upper arm and grasp your own wrist. Drive forward and trip.

---

ful kick to your attacker's groin (see Figure 11.11). You can also use this crossed-arm defense to block an upward knife thrust.

You might also try a forearm block. With one of your forearms, block your attacker's forward-thrusting arm. Run your other hand under his upper arm and grasp your own wrist. Push forward, tripping your assailant (see Figure 11.12).

I don't recommend that you fight against a gun. But if you choose to try, your response must be immediate and very certain. Step to the outside of the gun, and hit with a pug hand forcefully into the arm holding the gun, causing the gun to swing away. If your attacker drops the gun, send a kick to his knee (see Figure 11.13).

Multiple Attackers

If you should be attacked by more than one person, remember the same principles. Pray quickly first, then bite, grind, and hurt every

Figure 11.13 WEAPON ATTACKS: Gun

Step to the outside of the gun.

Pug hand strike the arm holding the gun, causing the gun to swing away.

Lean away and kick to the knee.

Figure 11.14 MULTIPLE ATTACKERS: Two from the Front

available part on your attackers. Kick whichever attacker is closest to you.

A good principle for fighting against two people is to take them one at a time. If they are both heading toward you from the front, quickly step to the side of the closest one, so that you are in a straight line with them. Then deal with the closest one first (see Figure 11.14).

If the two attackers are at your sides, holding you or pulling you in both directions, figure out which is pulling you harder and then pull with your weight in that direction. Kick the closest attacker in the knee, stomach, or groin. Then go for the knee of the other with a "T" kick (see Figure 11.15).

If one attacker is holding you in a bear hug from behind, and the other is coming toward you from the front, keep your cool.

Figure 11.15 MULTIPLE ATTACKERS: Two Pulling in Opposite Directions

Figure 11.16 MULTIPLE ATTACKERS: Bear Hug and Oncoming Attack

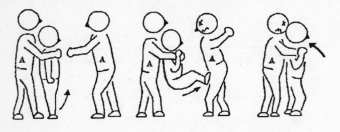

Wait until the oncoming attacker is within range, then grasp the arms of the one that is holding you and draw your legs up. Snap a hard kick in the approaching attacker's face, groin, or stomach. Butt your head into the face of the attacker behind you (see Figure 11.16).

Getting Out of There

No matter what attack situation you find yourself in, your goal is to get out of there! There are some principles that can help you make a run for it.

When the moment of opportunity for escape arrives, get your body going fast in the right direction. First turn your head in the direction of escape; your body will follow! Take a short step with the leg that is farthest from the attacker, and lean forward over that front leg. Pump your arms vigorously. Get moving, and don't look back!

Practice escaping with a partner who is about two feet from you. Try to turn and run to a specific spot without being touched. Practicing this exercise may save your life someday.

12

With God's Help You Can Do It!

*A*LTHOUGH I HAVE TAUGHT SELF-DEFENSE SKILLS IN conjunction with physical education for twenty-five years, I didn't really understand the depth of the problem of assault and rape against women until recent years. The physical skills were fun, and the class fulfilled a general physical education requirement at the college where I teach. But it wasn't until I began to study the roots of the problem of defense for women that it became a personal mission to understand the "whys."

Early on I went to the Lord and asked *why* women had this problem. Where did it come from? Would it ever be resolved? I searched the Scriptures as far back as Old Testament times, when the stage was set to shape the view and value of women. I discovered that the sin of domination and abuse had its root in that terrible day in the garden when the first people disobeyed the Lord. I traced the pattern through time to the present, and it was disheartening to realize that the enduring problem of the use and abuse of women was not going to go away. The devaluation of women even lies hidden under the cloak of so-called Christianity in far too many churches. The Church sends a woman conflicting messages: that she must accept domination as part of her Christian responsibility and that she is a loved and gifted person before the Lord.

The Great Liberator

There came a point when I tearfully asked God, "Does it matter to you that I am a woman? Are my talents, ideas, and dreams less than someone else's because they reside in a female body?" His response was overwhelming. I felt his love and warmth fill me, and at that moment I began to regard myself with value. At the same time, a realization of right and responsibility for who I was and my need to protect myself dawned on me. I was suddenly freed by Jesus, the great liberator! You can discover self worth when you see yourself through the eyes of God. And how you begin to feel about what God created when he made you will change the way you feel about defending yourself.

Once I realized that the problems of domination, assault, rape, brutalization, and murder would always be there for women, I sought the Lord again—this time for a solution. As we stand before God seeking the truth, we recognize that every problem has a solution, and God, invited by the victim, can be part of that solution to the problem of the devaluation and assault of women. We depend on these truths: God loves each woman, he hates brutalization, and he gives power to those who call on him. And we also know that a frightened woman is a physically powerful woman, and a practiced woman can be an effective force in defense.

Free to Fight Back

We have talked about many possible situations in this book. And we have talked quite a bit about preventative measures of defense. I've given you some guidelines to develop an awareness system which promptly provides an "Uh-oh" feeling when your circumstances are suspect. This system will help you to avoid or escape potentially threatening situations. The tricky part is developing this awareness without becoming paranoid and fearful, without constantly looking over your shoulder. It helps to know that once you develop your system, your actions and awareness will become habitual, not so much on a conscious level.

I am often asked, "Won't the attacker just get more angry with me if I try to hurt him?" He may be pretty angry anyway! I will never believe that doing nothing is better than doing something. Usually an attacker is bent on harming you; you may even be facing brutality or murder. Feel free to fight back! It is your right, and your proficient skills will help you strike a disabling blow.

Remember that when you are trapped, you are fighting for *space and time to escape.* When you practice, you may be tempted to focus mainly on the escape skills because they seem less violent. But most attackers don't give up so easily; escaping his grasp is not enough. Plan to deliver an incapacitating injury and then escape. You can't be expected to stay around and battle an attacker to the ground. Your goal is to *incapacitate,* to keep him from coming after you. One strike or blow may not do the job, so be prepared to use every available part of your body for repeated blows. If you can only get one shot, make it your best one!

Maybe you're feeling overwhelmed by all the maneuvers and blows we've covered. If so, work on just a few and do them well!

Concentrate on the eyes, throat, and groin since these are the most vulnerable parts of any person's body. Do each movement slowly and accurately at first—it's better to be on target than fast. Your speed will increase with practice.

You Can Do It!

I wish that all the guidelines in this book could guarantee you freedom from assault. But they can't—not any more than taking driving lessons can guarantee freedom from car accidents. But you do not jump into a car and drive away without having had lessons, or into the deep end of the pool to do a backstroke without swimming lessons. Because assault is always a possibility in any place and at any time, we need to have *lessons* in handling an assault.

The one guarantee I can promise is that God loves you and will be with you in every circumstance. He will hear your desperate call. So call on his name first; then his power and your physical force will make you a formidable foe to any attacker.

Love, worth, power, freedom. Remember that God values and delights in each of his people. He doesn't want his creation abused. You are free to fight back; you can choose not to be a victim.

Bibliography

Banks, Aaron (Department of the Army Manual). *Green Beret Combatives for Self-Defense*. New York: Parallax Publishing Company, 1967.

Bullard, Lt. Jim. *Looking Forward to Being Attacked*. Memphis, TN: Memphis Police Department, 1977.

Conroy, Mary, and Edward Ritvo. *Common Sense Self-Defense*. St. Louis, MO: C.V. Mosby Company, 1977.

Daeshik, Kim. *Judo*. Dubuque, IA: William C. Brown, 1969.

Ellison, Bob, and Jill Shipstad. *This Book Can Save Your Life*. New York: New American Library, 1968.

Farkas, Emil, and Margaret Leeds. *Fight Back: A Women's Guide to Self Defense*. New York: Holt, Rhinehart, and Winston, 1978.

Gambordella, Theodore, Ph.D. *Seven Days to Self-Defense*. Chicago: Contemporary Books, Inc., 1980.

Griffith, Liddon. *Mugging: You Can Protect Yourself*. Englewood Cliffs, NJ: Prentice-Hall, Inc., 1978.

Gustafson, Donald and Linda Masaki. *Self-Defense for Women*. Boston: Allyn & Bacon, Inc., 1970.

Heyden, S. Margaret, and Allen Tarpenning. *Personal Defense for Women*. Belmont, CA: Wadsworth, 1970.

Lomack, Craig. *How to Protect Yourself with Karate*. New York: Pocket Books, 1966.

Monkerud, Donald, and Mary Heiny. *Self-Defense for Women*. Dubuque, IA: William C. Brown, 1980.

Offstein, Jerrold. *Self-Defense for Women*. Palo Alto, CA: National Press Books, 1972.

Pickering, Michael. *A Women's Self-Defense Manual*. Mountain View, CA: World Publications, Inc., 1979.

Seidler, Armond. *Defend Yourself: Scientific Personal Defense*. Boston: Houghton Mifflin, 1978.

Stock, F. Patricia. *Personal Safety and Defense for Women*. Minneapolis: Burgess Publishing Company, 1968.

Tegner, Bruce. *Bruce Tegner's Complete Book of Self-Defense. Second Edition.* New York: Bantam Books, 1965.

Tegner, Bruce. *Instant Self-Defense.* New York: Grosset & Dunlap, 1965.

Tegner, Bruce, and Alice McGrath. *Self-Defense for Girls.* New York: Bantam Books, 1969.

Tegner, Bruce. *Self-Defense for Women: A Simple Method.* Thor Publishing Company, nd.

Wyness, G.B. "Jerry." *Practical Personal Defense.* Palo Alto, CA: Mayfield Publishing Company, 1975.